The Way I See It

See It

Fiction * Philosophy * Soul Food

We ... Are Here!

Think about it ... dear Reader ...

As you read this page ... *you* ... and every other human being, are standing on a HUGE sphere of rock and water, called *Earth*. It is 24,901 miles (40,075 Km) , in circumference. It is hurtling through the negative 457 degree F (negative 270 C), freezing cold vacuum of space, at 67,000 MPH (107,826 KPH). That's 18.5 miles (29.77 Km) ... *per second* ... <u>every</u> single second of your life!

This planet we call home ... and *all* of the 7.7 *billion* of us on it, completely circle the Sun, once a year; traveling a distance of 584 million miles (940 million Km). We humans control absolutely *none* of this. All we can do ... is *be* here.

Tell me, dear Reader ... How big do you feel, *right now*?

~Jeff Gaines

Cover Photo by: Jeff Gaines © 2018

Printed in the United States of America

First Printing, 2018

First Edition

Series Debut

ISBN: 978-1-7335377-0-4

Published by Jeff Gaines

Author's Website:

www.JeffGaines.world

Author Instagram:

www.instagram.com/thatrascalmerlin

Credits for all quotes and lyrics used within this book under fair use are listed at the end of the book.

"Which man can save
his brother's soul?
Oh man, it's about self control.
Don't gain the world
and lose your soul.
Wisdom is better
than silver or gold."

~Robert Nesta Marley
From the Bob Marley and The Wailers Title: "Zion Train"

For Gen Gen ...

Whether or not I've ever told you this, I simply can't remember. But, there is something I really want you to know ... I learned that I could wear my heart on my sleeve ... from *you*.

I was always fascinated by how confidently you could do this in front of people. More so, with how you could do it with such passion. In your own words, it is "Empowering" ... "Freeing" ... and more importantly, "... It might even help someone else along the way".

On the evening that I'd asked you about this in front of the Bowery Ballroom and you gave me that answer, I thought about it on the train all the way home to Brooklyn, and it has stuck with me forever. I will always admire you for bestowing me with this new confidence and will be forever thankful to you for passing it along to me.

Never let it be said that "You can't teach an old dog new tricks" ... For I am living proof that you can.

You ... on no uncertain terms, are the reason this book exists.

Before learning this from you, I was too old, too private, too proud and just plain too Aries stubborn to ever show most of these writings to the public. Showing them to a friend or two is one thing ... Sharing them with the world ... is truly wearing your heart upon your sleeve. And *you* my dear, are the perfect Hero from whom to have learned this ability.

Biggest Love,

Jeff

No Man is an Island

*"No man is an island entire of itself; every man
is a piece of the continent, a part of the main;
if a clod be washed away by the sea, Europe
is the less, as well as if a promontory were, as
well as any manner of thy friends or of thine
own were; any man's death diminishes me,
because I am involved in mankind.
And therefore never send to know for whom
the bell tolls; it tolls for thee."*

MEDITATION XVII
Devotions upon Emergent Occasions
John Donne
Originally Published in 1694

Table Of Contents

Many, *Many* Thanks ...

Oh good grief, where do I even *begin*?

I guess Hello Poetry is as good a place as any ...

The friends I have made there are priceless. Their love and comments about my posts (no matter *how* outside of the box I was), were the final push that made me publish this book. Hell, I had begun writing in the early 1990's! But it wasn't until a friend gave me a chunk of her courage, that I actually began to compile it as a book. Then ... it took *another* 9 years to get it together. Admittedly, I have written some great stuff and ideas to add to it during that time; but I do tend to put things off if I think they are not *perfect*.

Silly, I know.

Mea maxima culpa.

Well, after seeing the reactions to my uploads there ... after all the love shown to me and my precious words ... I *knew* that I had no more excuses. I knew it was time to put up, or shut up. I have a few over 150 followers there. I hope I don't let them down with this book. Most of it was on Hello Poetry and they have read it. I had to remove it from there in order to publish it. It felt like leaving home. I kinda felt like I was betraying them somehow. I still read and interact there though. I could never just leave there altogether.

I can't name them all here, because if I claim to, then miss any, I have done a disservice. So I won't even try. If you are one of my followers or readers ... THANK YOU for all your love, your reads and support!

There are some absolutely mind-blowing writers to be found there and I have also made some dear friends as well ... some people, I even chat with outside of the site. These people have all touched me in their own ways and that is between them and I. But, I still want to thank some of them, in no certain order ...

Kim Johanna Baker: Thank you *ever* so much for all the love, sunshine and insightful comments on my work. You helped me so much more than you'll

EVER know and I can NOT thank you enough. Your poetry, like you … is purely spiritual, eloquent and simply timeless. Bless you, my love.

Cné: Meeting you and making a new friend … in you, and now your husband, has really sweetened my life. Strange how close folks can get before ever meeting face to face. It has been a wonderful adventure. I love our hours on the phone. They mean the world to me. *Too* fun … as long as you don't miss your exit!

Heart of Silver: Such an odd feeling I had when we first met. All wrong, but odd, nonetheless. Still, I am so glad that I met you. I really love our conversations … your cookies … your comments *and* your writings!

Temporal Fugue: The brother-from-another-mother that can rhyme about nearly anything … and do it *well*. Your rhyming reviews and your poetry have been such a great breath of fresh air and I am so glad that we have become friends. The way you look at things, from your very own angle, is really enjoyable.

Melissa S.: Having a pal like you here in Alabama makes me feel right at home. Your warm encouragement has pushed me even harder. I can not thank you enough. I can't wait for the first meeting of the "Lower Alabama Poetry Collective"! Your writing brings a nice element of "lovely" to HePo.

TSPoetry: Your wit and your prose are two edges of a very polished sword. I always look forward to your takes on my uploads. Thanks man, for all the insight and the writes.

Haiku Donna: Oh Donna, your poems are so beautiful and I love the visions they conjure of your life with your beautiful family in Alaska. Thank you for introducing us all to those beautiful scenes of that mystical state and your family's adventures there. They are nothing less than wonderful, as are your comments about my own writings … I love them nearly as much!

Mary Gay Kearns: To know you … to speak to you across the pond on Skype … To read your words and see your paintings … all of it has had such a profound effect on me. I *dream* of the day that I can see your paintings, and you, before my very eyes. Finding you was one of my favorite things about being asked to join Hello Poetry. The places and times you have brought all of us to with your words are truly magical.

Jamadhi Verse: Always one of the deeper, faster rivers on HePo. The way you tune in to something I've written shakes my soul sometimes. You have such a brilliant mind and beautiful soul. Thanks JV.

Nylee: I love your out of the box look ... at *everything*! Your comments always warm my heart and I really want to thank you for them. They mean the world to me.

Angela: Chatting with you and getting to know you a bit was very unexpected ... and surprises are always the best when they contain apparitions like you. Such a free thinker. Such a free Spirit. I admire you and your work. I also love your comments, especially when they question me. You always make me think.

Medusa: If I am "El Jefe", then *you* are "El Presidente". Your lyrical writes and witty, insightful comments always make me smile. I love your genuine, heartfelt persona. Thank you, my sweet.

Traveler: Our shared passion of dogs speaks so much about us. Your writing is always challenging and often deeper than a Great Lake ... as are some of your comments on my writings. Thanks, my Brutha.

Carina: Meeting you injected me with a bit of your lively youth. Your old soul flows with "deeper-than-should-be-written-by-someone-so-young" prose. I can not wait to watch as you age, like a wine, and bring us all some of the greatest poetry in the world. Your reviews have moved my very soul. Thanks Carina.

And last, but not least ... Ashley Kocher: The undisputed world record holder for composing poetry on a cell phone. A *lot* of it! At *least* one a day! *ALL* of it, really good. So, so amazing. Thanks for your support.

I also want to thank Budvido for pushing me along with encouragement as well as all my family and friends that have, through the years, read my work or shown me support. I know some of you aren't really readers and did this out of love. It didn't go unnoticed ... *or* unappreciated. Thank you so very much. It is my hope, that I have made any and all of you proud ... in one way ... or another ... Especially *you*, Mum.

My arms really are big enough to hug you all ...
Believe it.

~*Jeff*

On Being Receptive ...

"In my adventures ...
All of my travels ...
In all of my interactions with others ...
and all of the experiences that have been brought to me ...
If there is one thing that I have learned ...
It is that the more receptive I am ...
The more things I receive."

~Jeff Gaines

Hello, dear Reader!

I'm Jeff Gaines ... It is very nice to meet you.

I can't thank you enough for picking up my first book. I hope this thing that you hold in your hands, be it paper back or digital words on a screen ... and you ... truly find each other. I hope that it helps you find something not only within yourself ... but those in the world around you as well. I'm going to attempt this rather lofty accomplishment with a few fictional short stories, a handful of personal essays about events or moments in my life and how they effected me, and a collection of my poetry along with some of the stories about, or behind, the pieces.

It's a bit of a "sampler", if you will .. a look at a few of my genres. My way of introducing my writing and what I am about when I write most anything. More often than not, I write about me ... *Therefore* ... I write about *us.* I am, we are.

I know, I know ... believe me ... I hear you ...

"What the ...?"

"Who puts all these genres in one book and attempts to pull them together somehow?"

Well ... in a word ... ME. I don't believe in thinking outside the box ... In fact, I don't have a box ... and you shouldn't either. Boxes *contain* things ... *protect* them even. You can't *discover* things from a box.

I'm going to show you things within most, or should I say, many of us all. I'm going to show you things within yourself ... and much of it will be done by showing you how I found these things in myself through my adventures. Believe me, my life has been an adventure, as you will soon see as we get to know each other through my books. I've met, worked with and interacted with *countless* people around the world.

Poor people, rich people, stars of Film, TV and Music ... even criminals. Good, bad *and* indifferent. But ... *my* adventure isn't what this collection is really about ... as I said ... it's about adventuring into *us* ... *into everybody.* I hope that by letting you have a look deep inside me, you might see something inside yourself. Or, perhaps, that something I have observed will help you understand something in those around you as well. After all, we're just beings roaming a huge sphere, hurtling through space. We *need* to understand *us.*

It has been said that it's not the destination, but the journey itself, that is important. I only half agree, because I believe that *both* are equally important. The trick, the way I've come to see it in my heart anyway, is realizing that it isn't one singular destination that we all strive towards … it is an endless series of them.

And the journey?

Well, it never ends … in the world we all roam in … *or* our lives.

I also hope that my fictional characters move you, scare you, enrage you, even pull at your heartstrings … because each and every one of them could be you or someone that you know or love. Or, they could be someone that you miss, someone that means something to you or perhaps even someone that you hate.

Recognition … That's my goal here. To help you recognize that all of us, including *you*, are people … each as unique *and* alike as the other. Some more extreme than others. Some more pensive than others.

Yet still … all alike when it comes right down to it. Omnibus idem. You may or may not share some or even all of my philosophies, but I do believe that you will find many things here in me … especially *you*.

Oh … and you *might* even learn a little Latin!

~*Jeff*

Glossary of Terms

Glossary of Terms

Seriously?

Did you actually just *fall* for that, dear Reader?

Wow …

As if this book isn't compound enough … A Glossary of Terms?

Really?

Besides … *those* go in the *back* of a book!

Sheesh!

From Thee Edge

"Come to the edge," he said.
"We can't, we're afraid!" they responded.
"Come to the edge," he said.
"We can't, We will fall!" they responded.
"Come to the edge," he said.
And so they came.
And he pushed them.
And they flew."

~Guillaume Apollinaire

French Poet and Philosopher

"I want to stand as close to the edge as I can without going over. Out on the edge you see all kinds of things you can't see from the center."

~From the title: "Player Piano" by Kurt Vonnegut

Bum Leg

There was no sun today. As I walked across the driveway to the barn and looked out over the fields and our farmhouse, I couldn't see sunlight on anything. I watched the corn flutter in the breeze and it took me back to a day that seems like yesterday. I've been writing now for almost twenty years and though I've thought about putting this on paper umpteen million times; I've never had the courage. To this day, I don't know if I was dreaming or if I actually had a real-life miracle. One thing is for sure … It *felt* real … *and* it changed my life forever. Besides all that, I'm not too sure that anyone would believe me anyway. I know my Dad *tried* to believe me. The only *real* proof I have is my Papaw's old pocket watch … *and* the note.

At any rate, I'll tell this tale now and when I'm gone, maybe someone will get a kick out of it or maybe it'll make them think … the way it did me. I won't even try to pass it off to my agent or my publisher. I *like* my job. I love working the farm to this day, but the income from writing keeps me from having to worry about what will happen when I take my harvest to market … like my Dad did all too often. As did his Dad before him. As have all farmers for that matter. These men have gambled with their lives, farms and families for their very existence for far too long.

It all started about a month or so before harvest, when I was fourteen years old. That previous winter, right after the first hard snow, my Mom and my Papaw were on their way into town to get candles and kerosene for the lamps. It had been especially windy that season and we were without lights more often than not. You see, our farm stood alone almost thirty miles from any other farm. At the time, we were also alone on our power grid. It was one of the first farms outside Sioux City to have electricity.

One of the wires, legs as they're called, that traveled out to our place from the power station was loose on one of the poles. So, whenever the wind got too high, it would shake the line causing a short and some of the lights in our farmhouse would flicker, sometimes popping a bulb or worse still, a fuse. The frustrated Power Company searched a whole summer in vain for the loose connection. While it wasn't cost effective to check all sixty miles of poles, they found and replaced a questionable transformer with a newer model … *all* to no avail.

The very next time we had some big winds, we went through half a box of fuses. My Dad and My Pap went to the board of directors at Mid-west Power and Light to plead for a resolve, but they walked away instead with a mutual agreement. They weren't too enthused … but it was better than nothing. The Power Company agreed to supply us with a lifetime supply of fuses and a monthly allotment of bulbs. It was better than nothing … I guess.

Well, we had gone through all the bulbs that month already and my Pap was doing a lot of tinkering that winter. He wanted candles for his workbench. As he and my Mom were going down Route Sixty-three, they came over the hill at the railroad crossing and didn't see the Noon train that was making its way into town. The police said that by the time he hit the brakes on his old truck, it was too late. The road was too icy and they slid right in front of the train. Christmas just wasn't the same that year.

I remember sitting in my Pap's big chair, holding my Christmas stocking. I stared into the fire and listened to the cold Iowa wind outside. I wished that my Mom and my Pap would walk through the door and give me big hugs and kisses. I wished that I could wake up from this bad dream. But … I was all too awake. The only thing that made that day bearable was the look on my Granny's face when she unwrapped the cane I had carved for her. My Pap and my Dad were both carvers. I remember watching them carve everything from serving plates and furniture to tobacco pipes.

We would all giggle after my Mom would give them what-for about all the shavings on the porch. I was just fascinated by their talent. When I turned ten, they gave me my first whittling knife. I started to carve a piece of wood and when I was done, I had nothing left to carve. I was just so excited to be carving like them. My Pap looked at the sliver of wood that was left from what started as a stick and he grinned from ear to ear. Looking at it as serious as he could he asked me kindly "What'cha got there boy?"

I remember looking at it and then answering him as serious as I could "It's a toothpick for my Mom!" I announced. He took it from my hand and began sanding it smooth. He smiled at me as proud as could be.

"And a fine toothpick it is too … A fine toothpick." Well, four years and countless tree limbs later, I had become a wood carver almost on the level of my tutors. At least that's what they told me anyway. I had worked secretly on my Granny's cane in the barn until it got too cold, then I finished it on my Pap's bench in the basement. I tapped, chipped, chiseled, sanded and painted until my hands were numb. She pulled the paper from it so carefully I almost screamed in anticipation. She *never* tore her Christmas wrappings; she saved them. "Waste not, want not." She would say. She held my work up to the firelight and looked through the rims of her round reading glasses at the intricate leaves and flowers I had worked so hard to inlay in the wood.

The appreciation on her face made all those hours so much more than worth it ... and in those moments after she took it out of its wrappings, I felt the weight of my loss lifted from my soul. Adding to my joy, she handed it to my Dad. He inspected it with genuine amazement. He looked at me with a look on his face that I hadn't seen before. When I look back now, I realize that it was *his* sense of loss ... for *me*. He told me it was the finest piece of whittling he'd ever seen. I felt like a man that cold Christmas morning, but it was the upcoming planting season that would usher in my manhood ... *and* my understanding of life ... Good or bad.

My Dad and I had been out surveying our freshly planted rows of corn. The sun was warm that day and the breeze almost tingled as it drifted over the little beads of sweat on my forehead. I felt so proud to be my Dad's understudy. Before this, I had been the "farmhand" of the family; feeding chickens and helping my Mom and my Granny doing the menial tasks that never seem to end around a working farm. I couldn't wait for the day when I could go out and operate tractors and combines ... I just *knew* it would make me a man.

Well, I got my wish, *but* as life usually does you, *not* in the way I'd imagined it would come. After my Pap died, I had to do *both* of the tasks, chores in the morning and working the fields in the afternoon. My Dad had taught me how to operate the tractor, as promised, right after my thirteenth birthday. As he and my Pap harvested the corn that year, I would follow the combine so that I could practice staying in between the rows. My Dad stood on the back of the combine watching the corn being sprayed from the hopper ... *and* watching me battling to keep the wheels straight. Learning was one thing, but now I was doing it for *real*.

Satisfied that our crop was sound, we headed back to the smell of one of my Granny's famous Pot Roast's. The smell was like the call of a siren. After you'd eaten it once, you couldn't control yourself if you smelled that smell again. Our walk from the barn slowly turned to a laughing foot-race as we got closer to that kitchen she was so effortlessly turning into a farm boy's nirvana. My Dad beat me to the steps, but I jumped up the three steps in one bound and to the door in another, triumphantly sneering at him as I swung open the door and filled my nose with her roast beef heaven. She grinned at our competition and rushed us away from the counter to go and wash our hands.

"Off with you, now!" She commanded, "There'll be no nibblin' 'til yer hands is warshed!" Her Kentucky accent always warmed my heart ... I loved that woman in a way that can't be described. Of all the people in my life, even my parents, I never felt like anybody could see through my soul like she could. She knew just how to make me smile when I was sad ... She knew just how to correct me when I was wrong ... But, most of all, she knew just how to praise me when I'd done something right. Making her proud was the greatest feeling I've ever known … When she squeezed me as she gave me approval, I felt like I could do anything. I also felt like I'd do anything to get that hug. There's never been anyone else like her in my life.

We were sitting at the table eating our supper; my Granny pulled my Pap's old pocket watch out of her apron and pressed the crown to open it up. After she read the time, she looked at me with a grin, "So Jefferson, would you like to drive over to the feed store with me after dinner?" I was nodding with my mouth full, I knew what she *really* wanted to take me along for. "I had Ben leave us some chicken feed out on the loading dock and if we're gonna have eggs next week we'll be needin' to go and pick it up." True, she did need me to pick up the heavy bags of feed, but the *real* reason that she wanted to take me along … was a driving lesson!

My Dad wanted to wait to teach me to drive a car. He said that teaching me the tractor *and* the car in one season was more than his heart could handle. She saw my frustration … as was her way … and started sneaking me off for lessons every chance she got. But today, something else had caught my attention … Something that I'd had in the back of my mind for some time now. I had admired that watch since the day my Pap had taught me how to tell time on it. After he died, I began to have hopes of someday having it for my very own. Today, I decided to try and reinforce my wishes by asking her if she remembered telling me that she would give it to me one day.

Looking across the table at me, my Dad told me, on no uncertain terms, that that pocket watch would be *his* long before it would *ever* be mine. I didn't realize it then, but the reason she didn't say anything to his statement was because he was teasing me. After I got up and ran away to my room for a cry, she chastised him for teasing me. He told her that if I was gonna grow up to run "His" farm, that I was going to have to have a lot thicker skin than that. She told me this as she gave me my lesson that day. I remember not totally believing her … I *also* remember her trying to hide her nervousness at my inability to keep the car on the windy road. The fields were all fresh planted, so there was nothing to block the stiff, Iowa wind. Even though I knew she would never lie to me, I still felt like my Dad was really mean at the dinner table.

When we got back, I put the feed in the shed and she let me park the car in the barn. As I got up to the porch, they tried to hide their spat about her letting me park the car. I pretended like I didn't hear them. We went inside and I helped her get up the stairs so she could sit in her room and read. The wind was playing havoc on the lights as usual, but in her room, they didn't flicker. Actually, they only flickered in the entry hall, the living room, the kitchen, the dining room, and the basement. Those circuits were on the bad leg.

My Dad was in the living room rewinding a coil for one of the pump motors. We had found the south field dry that afternoon and it only took a minute for my Dad to find the problem. He told me he'd need to fix it tonight and have the pump going tomorrow or our freshly planted maize would wither and die. I knew he could fix it, he could fix anything. It was a trait that he'd picked up from my Pap. I hoped that one day I would inherit this great gift. He thanked me for helping my Granny up the steps, but he *didn't* apologize for teasing me at dinner. I didn't mind helping her though; I'd do anything for her.

She had always limped, at least as long as I could remember. My Dad told me his mother had fallen down a flight of steps in her youth. Since that accident, she had always had a bum leg. I swear though … I *never* heard her complain once. Even when it was cold and her face showed the extra effort it took for her to walk, she always smiled.

I went into the kitchen to make some popcorn. As I shook the cast iron kettle, the lights began to flicker and then went out altogether. I pulled the kettle from the burner and ran down to the basement fuse box. I'd done it so many times that I didn't need the flashlight. After finding and lighting a candle, I fumbled across my Pap's workbench for the paper box of fuses. It was the next to the last one. After I swapped them out, the lights came on in the basement.

My eyes gazed across the dusty old bench and I pictured my Pap fixing my bicycle … or my Mom's toaster. He was amazing. When he wasn't fixing something, he was baking cookies. He never cooked anything else … just chocolate chip cookies. He said they soothed the souls of young and old alike. After he died, we didn't come down here much; just to change fuses mostly. I ran back up the steps to the kitchen and went back to my popcorn. When it was done, I poured it into two bowls and headed back to the living room. I set my Dad's bowl on the coffee table, then sat up on my Granny's organ bench to watch him work.

When he finished, he put the pump-motor back together and ran me off upstairs to get a bath and go to bed. I had a lot to do before I went to school the next morning and four-thirty a.m. was going to come awful quick. I didn't argue, I knew he was right. I gave him a hug and ambled up the stairs. When I woke up in the morning, I immediately noticed something was wrong. As I got to the top of the steps, something was missing. It wasn't 'til I got to the kitchen that I realized what it was. I didn't smell my Granny's biscuits … Or her ham … or her red-eye gravy.

My Dad was making coffee and I asked him where my Granny was. He kind of gave me a dirty look and shook his head. "Your Grandmother is seventy-four years old. Maybe she's tired." I didn't say a thing. He always was a grump in the morning. I let out a long sigh and began scanning around the counter for some bread or leftover biscuits. He gave me another dirty look. I could feel his demeanor all the way across the room. "I s'pose you want someone to cook yer breakfast fer ya."

I acted as nonchalant as I could. "No, I'm gonna have me a peanut butter and molasses sandwich." I informed him. He poured me a glass of milk and reminded me of everything I needed to do before I left.

As I fed the chickens, I kept my eye on my Granny's window. I slopped the hogs, watered the dogs and checked the hen house. I took the eggs back to the house and was surprised to see that the light in her room still wasn't on. I rode my bike out to where my Dad was fixing the pump and he gave me a ride to the schoolhouse. It wasn't until they came and got me out of class that the funny feeling I had had in my belly all morning was explained. My Granny had passed away in her sleep. As I cried in the truck on the way back to the farm, my Dad told me that I had only today, and the day of the funeral, to cry. He said he wouldn't stand for me to cry after that. He told me that I was too big to cry any more.

I was so hurt and angry that I yelled at him through my tears. "NO" … " I screamed. " … YOU'RE the one that's too big to cry!" I remember him looking over at me in amazement. I looked back at him and finished with "You DIDN'T cry when Mommy died and you probably WON'T cry now!"

He whipped the truck over onto the side of the road … but instead of the whoopin' I just *knew* was coming; he looked at me in total silence. It was *worse* than a whoopin'. He shut off the motor and stared out the windshield. After a while, I just couldn't look at him. He said, "Jefferson Robles … If you think, for one moment, that I didn't cry when your mother was taken away from us …" He took a huge, deep breath and let it out with a sigh. "YOU are sadly mistaken." He took his "Red Rose Feed" cap off and laid his head against the back window. His eyes were closed. "I'm a grown man …" He said. " … I have a lot of responsibility … I know it's hard for a boy your age to understand now, but I just can't be cryin' in front of the whole world. It makes me look weak."

He was right … I *didn't* understand. That ride home was almost as long as the painful ride home from the funeral. The service was beautiful, but nothing was going to make me stop crying. I was waiting for him to come and tell me to stop, but he didn't. He went up to his room without a word. I remember looking around at all my relatives as they flooded my house with stories about my

Granny. I didn't hear a word they said. I was in my own world … and it was shattered. It was bad enough that I lost my Mom *and* my Pap both at one time.

Even then, I had my Granny to help me through it. But now … what did I have? My Dad didn't even want me to cry. I shook uncontrollably as I pondered what my life was about to become and as soon as it dawned on me that I'd never see her smiling face cooking breakfast like I had every other morning of my life; something in me snapped. I felt like the whole world had ganged up on me. I never cried about her after that day. In fact … I didn't cry again until the day my father died.

Okay … There was *one* other time, but I'm getting to that …

That summer, after my Granny left us, my father and I worked on the farm twelve to fifteen hours a day. He was different and so was I. I tried to make him happy and do everything he told me; but it seemed he was never satisfied. I remember going to bed filled with frustration many times that summer. I don't think either of us realized how frustrated we both were *and* how much we were missing our family. Like father, like son … I doubt either of us would have admitted it. Still, I felt hopeless. I felt like my Dad was taking his frustration out on me. I even told him one afternoon, in the middle of one of our arguments, that he should have taught me how to run the equipment sooner. That way, I could have been more helpful. He just looked at me and shook his head. I was too young to understand … he was too old to make the best of the situation and have some patience.

At the end of the summer, he and I were sitting at the table eating dinner. I was thinking about how much I missed my Granny's cooking when he asked me what time it was. I looked into the living room at the huge Grandfather clock that stood between the fireplace and my Granny's old organ. As I turned back to tell him what time it was, I had a flash of my Granny looking at my Pap's pocket watch.

My heart fluttered.

I looked at my Dad and he at me. He must have noticed the strange look on my face as I looked at him. I was trying to sum up my words. "What?" Was all he said. I bit my lip, gathered up my courage and popped the question … "Dad, whatever happened to Papaw's pocket watch?" His face grew puzzled. He looked down at the table and shook his head.

"You know, come to think of it … I don't know." My heart sank. His promise that the watch would be his before it was mine replayed in my head. My teeth gritted. I just *knew* he had that watch. I stared him down. "You mean you don't know where it is?" He looked at his half empty plate.

"No son, I don't."

He moved his peas around with his fork then raised his eyes up to mine … "We'll look around for it after dinner."

I *knew* he was lying … and I *knew* we would never find that watch.

I was right … Mostly … But I'll get to that too.

We looked all through her room and then the rest of the house. We even looked in the car. I told him it was in her apron when she went to bed that night. He said, "Well, it's not in there now, I washed that apron and put it away a long time ago." Again, my teeth gritted. I *hated* him at that moment. I was *sure* that he had that watch … *My* watch. I screamed at him that I knew he had it. I told him it was mine fair and square … my Granny *told* me I could have it and that he had no right to keep it from me.

I ran out of the house, jumped on my bike and rode all the way down to the railroad crossing. I didn't cry though. I was too mad to cry. I sat at that crossing until I started to fall asleep. I was hoping a train would come. I could jump on it and just leave this place forever. My Dad, the farm, the corn, the chickens … everything. I thought I could join the circus or maybe go into the Army like my Papaw did when he was fifteen. I listened to the wind blow through the rows of corn and the barbed-wire fences that were all around me. I looked up and down the tracks, finally putting my ear to the rail … Nothing.

After the moon started to set, I thought about my Dad getting worried. "Good!" I thought. "Let him worry; He doesn't care about my feelings!" I didn't want to leave anyway; I'd never seen the moon so big and so beautiful. Listening to the wind some more, I felt my eyelids start getting really heavy. The ride home wore me out. I went into the barn, climbed up into the cab of the combine and fell asleep.

A few hours later I woke to the sound of my Dad's voice; he was calling for me. I jumped up and opened the cab door, calling back to him. He slammed the barn door and chewed me up one side and down the other. He told me that I was grounded until my first report cards came out. That reminded me that school was about to start and my life was going to get even more complicated than it had ever been before. It was more than I could bear.

That year, our school had gotten buses. There wasn't one to pick me up way out on our farm, but, my Dad could drop me off at the Feed Store and a bus passed by there. The second week of school, I got on a friend's bus instead of my own and went to his house on the other side of the county. I stayed in his barn for almost two weeks, but it was starting to get cool at night. I knew that it wouldn't be too long before it would be too cold at night to stay there. Besides, soon his parents would start their harvest of hay and my safe hiding place wouldn't be so safe. One day, before his parents came home from town; he gave me his backpack filled with sandwiches and a blanket. I left his house and started heading south. I was going to go to Saint-Louis to try and join the Army.

I had only made it about a mile and a half down the road when a policeman pulled up behind me and figured out that I was a runaway. He took me home and my father thanked him and then looked at me with a disappointed pain. I ran to my room before he could say a word.

I hated my life …

I hated how my Dad was acting. He'd never treated me like this before my Granny died …

I missed my Mom … My Papaw … My Granny.

I wanted that watch.

I wanted things to be the way they used to be.

I wanted my Mom to take me to school.

I wanted my Pap to teach me how to build a fly lure.

I wanted my Dad to finish my combine driving lessons … but more than anything else …

I wanted my Granny to cook me breakfast …

I wanted to sit on the porch while she played her organ and sang until the dogs howled.

The frustration filled my belly like hardening cement.

My Dad didn't speak to me for days … weeks. I watched out my window as he and a few of my uncles began harvesting the corn. I wanted to help, but when I told him so … he looked at me shaking his head. I swore he had tears in his eyes … but he never cried … not my Dad. "No, no you don't, Son" was all he said. I watched him as he turned away and went out to the barn. Soon, all the corn would be harvested and he would have to go to market for at least three days to sell his crop. Someone would have to stay behind and take care of the animals … I *knew* who was going to get that job.

I started to think out a plan. I could run away again. But this time, I could get my stuff together, practice my driving and then take off in the car before he came back. I could surely make it to Saint-Louis that way. We had finally gotten a phone that previous summer, so, I could call him and tell him about the Army. He could come and get the car. Everyone would be happy.

At least that's how *I* saw it.

The day my father left for the market, the winter was beginning to show it's ugly head. The wind was blowing strong and steady. They left early so that they could take their time *and* so that none of the trucks would get blown off of the road. He and two of my uncles looked at the sky and wondered how long it would take them to get to the farmers market.

I looked at the sky and wondered how long I was going to have to practice my driving. As soon as I saw the last truck become a dot on the horizon, I ran out onto the porch. A giant bolt of lightning blinded me and the following crack of thunder scared me half out of my wits. I ran back into the kitchen and leaned against the counter. It was getting darker by the minute. I heard the first few drops of rain hitting the window and my tummy was rumbling like the thunder that was passing over the fields of my family's farm.

After I made a can of soup, I went into the living room and fell asleep to the sound of the rain. When I woke up, I took my bowl into the kitchen. I dropped it in the sink and reached for the dish soap. My Dad and my uncles had left a few dishes after their lunch. I figured I'd do them and then go to bed. Just as I got the water temperature right and plugged up the sink; the lights flickered once and then went out. I rolled my eyes and ran down to change the fuse. It was the last one in the box. I shook the box and looked around my Pap's bench.

There, on the top shelf, was an old box of fuses. They looked to be as old as my Pap. As I ran back up to my dishes, I wondered if they were any good. I would find out soon enough … For the next two days, as soon as the chores were done, I would take the car out and drive it around the farm.

I was getting pretty good and by the end of the second day, I wasn't stalling out on my take-offs and I was doing really good about keeping it in the middle of the road. Backing up was a little more difficult since I couldn't see very well over the huge seat of the old Dodge. I figured that as long as I didn't have to back up on the way to Saint-Louis, I'd be all right. Soon, I thought, I would be leaving this all behind.

I was sitting in the kitchen, waiting on my Dad's nightly call when the light's began flickering to the ever-rising wind outside the window. My Dad had said he'd be home tomorrow morning. They were supposed to leave tonight, but there was a big storm heading through, with the possibility for hail. When he called, he told me to make sure the animals were put up and to close the storm shutters. He said that they would leave in the morning and be back home by supper.

I remember thinking "He doesn't even care if I'm all right, he just wants his blessed animals put up and his stupid farmhouse closed up." I couldn't wait to leave the next morning. I fell into a daydream of shooting machine guns, throwing hand grenades and getting a tattoo.

As I started cutting a loaf of bread for sandwiches, I was trying to figure out how many I would need for my trip when the flickering lights turned to darkness … another fuse. The wind was howling something fierce. I could hear the big elm outside the front porch brushing against the house. The last time I had heard that, a tornado blew away our neighbor's whole barn. I had listened to the radio while I ate my dinner, but they didn't give a tornado warning, just a report of strong wind and rain coming in from the west. I sighed, thought about my sandwiches and headed for the basement. When I picked up the empty box … I shook it and remembered. Now, I wished I *had* brought the flashlight. I couldn't find a candle in the darkness.

I felt across the dusty, wood chip covered bench and up the wall. My fingertips found the old box of fuses. I pulled it down and held it against my belly with one hand while I dug around in it with the other. Too young and stubborn to go grab the flashlight, I hoped the one that I picked out was not only the right size but that it worked at all. I set down the box, pulled the old fuse and screwed in the one from the old box. The light in the basement flickered and my face was covered with a triumphant smile … for a moment.

The basement was filled with an almost eerie glow.

Instead of the usual blinding brightness of the sixty-watt bulb, I was standing in a dim, orange light. I let out a sigh of disappointment, thinking that I had installed either a bad fuse or one that was too weak.

I turned to start looking through the box for another one when a chill went straight up my spine.

My eyes, first open as big as silver dollars, then blinking in disbelief, gazed across the now pristine workbench. I looked on the floor for the wood chips … nothing. It was spic-and-span clean. The floor looked, even *smelled,* like it had just been painted. I bent over and looked under the bench.

Where there had once been a bin full of dirty, rusted carving and cutting tools thrown in total disarray … there were now just a few tools … all new … and totally laid out in order.

I stood up and looked around the basement. I started to shake. I still couldn't believe my eyes.

The whole basement was clean. There were no cobwebs ... I couldn't even smell the mildew that sometimes was so strong that it could make me sneeze.

The shelves where my Granny kept her homemade pickles and jams looked as spiffy as a shelf in Brewster's market. I walked over and picked up one of my favorites ... it was marked "Grape Jam". I caressed her handwriting on the white tape with my fingertips and I swear the jar felt like it was still warm. I was shaking my head in disbelief when my already strange experience ... became even stranger.

From upstairs, through the floorboards and joists that my Dad and my Pap had hand built and nailed into place all by themselves ... it came ...

The sound ... It drifted down over my body like one of my Granny's handmade quilts ...

The sound ...

The sound that had soothed me since I could remember ... was now making the hair on my arms and neck stand straight up, like a stalk of corn after a day of hard rain.

I listened for a few more moments ... it couldn't be ... it just *couldn't* be ...

I looked up at the floor above me ... and shivered.

Upstairs ...

I could hear my Granny's organ ...

At first, I thought maybe my Dad and my uncles were home ... and that they were playing a trick on me. I started to laugh at myself ... but only for a moment. The next thing I heard spun my mind into a tornado of confusion ... As I listened, my lips instinctively began to sing along ... It was my Granny ... singing "Onward Christian Soldiers".

For a moment ... I was scared.

But almost like my Granny was reassuring me with her voice, the fear fled my soul. I kept singing with her.

I thought for a moment that maybe I had shocked myself to death while I was changing the fuse ... Or that maybe I had fallen asleep in the kitchen while I waited for my Dad to call. I looked around the basement again ... still bathed in the weird, orange glow.

The music stopped for a minute ... and so did my heart. I jumped up and listened with all my might.

The light flickered for a moment and I swore I could hear my Pap grumbling from the kitchen. I put the nail from my thumb in my mouth, bit in and tore a piece of it right off. I spit it to the floor. I wiped my sweaty palms on my shirt, took a deep breath and headed toward the steps. As I got to the bottom of the steps, the sounds of the organ drifted down to me once again. Before I got to the top of the steps, she was singing … again.

I sang along … again.

"Yes … Jesus loves me … Yes … Jesus loves me … Yes … Jesus loves me … The bible tells me so."

When I got to the top of the stairs, the entryway seemed to be lit by the same dim light as the basement.

I took slow, short steps toward the front door. When I looked around I almost felt like I was lost.

The paint on the walls was different. It was green … my Granny's favorite color.

The old carpet at the front door was new. The brass knob of the front door was also shiny and new.

As I stepped on the carpet, I looked to my left into the kitchen … My mouth fell open …

There was my Papaw … taking cookies out of the oven with a big grin. They smelled incredible. I was about to go and have one of the fresh warm treats with him when the music stopped …

I spun around to look into the living room. Now I knew what treasure hunters felt like when they found some old pirate's buried loot …

This *had* to be that feeling.

I wanted to scream and just run to her …

But my legs … *and* my voice … were frozen.

It wasn't fear … I don't know *what* it was …

I just couldn't move …

I watched as my Granny grabbed the cane I had so lovingly carved for her and then slowly spun around on her organ bench. She smiled at me and suddenly a calmness fell over me that made me feel like I had just woke up from a long, refreshing sleep. She leaned the cane on the bench and patted her lap. I knew just what that meant. The smile on my face as I crossed that floor to sit on her lap went from one ear to the other. As I climbed up there, she squeezed me so tight I almost cried with joy. I squeezed her too and I didn't want to let go.

She gently wriggled my arms from around her and then her eyes found mine …

"Hello, Sweetie … you look good … really good. Yer a growin' like a weed"

"I miss you Granny" Was all I could say …

"Well, we miss you too, Deary."

I squeezed her again … She rubbed my back like she used to do when she tucked me in and put me to sleep. I closed my eyes and felt a tear of joy run down my cheek. She let go of me again and I leaned back.

She was holding me out almost at arm's length.

"Jefferson … Honey … I needed you to come here so we could talk."

I was nodding my head and she smiled at me. The light in the entrance hall flickered with the wind that was still howling from the storm outside. She bit her bottom lip as her thumbs caressed my biceps.

"Jefferson … yer a big boy now … an' I know you can understand what I'm a gonna say to ya … "

I was still nodding.

" … You know how our lights is always a flickerin'?"

"Yes, Granny?"

"Well, you've lived with that all your life … You know, most everybody else's lights don't do that."

"I know Granny."

"But you run down and change them fuses or climb up on a chair to change a bulb like it was nothin'."

"I know Granny … but it has to be done if we wanna see." She smiled at my statement and nodded her head as she continued. "That's right, but you don't complain … or rant and rave that it's unfair that you got ta do that … you just do it. I've watched ya and it makes me real proud."

I was grinning.

"Thanks, Granny, I love to make you proud." She pulled me in for another hug as she spoke.

"Well, you do … every day … you do. But that's not why I needed to see you tonight."

She leaned back again and looked at me with that proud smile that so warmed my soul.

"And I'm proud of you too, Granny … You never complain about your leg … even when it's cold."

She had big tears in her eyes … it made me cry too.

"That's right Honey, we all have some kinda bum leg we have to live with … you understand?"

I told her that I did … even though at that moment I don't think I did … completely.

"You see life ain't always fair … and life ain't always fun … And sometimes, it can hand you a bum leg. And whether it's a bum leg of electricity or your own bum leg, you just have to live with it. But if you go around makin' everybody miserable just because you ain't happy, well then everybody's miserable … Sometimes you have to just bite yer lip and go on … you see?"

I knew just what she meant. I *was* miserable … And so was my Dad.

We were making each other miserable.

"Yer Daddy loves you so very much …"

My eyes widened as I interrupted her. "He does not!" I took a trembling breath as I finished.

"He took Papaw's watch and he won't give it to me … I told him you said I could have it … but he says he don't know where it is." As I spoke, she was shaking her head with tears streaming down her face.

Those tears broke my heart.

"No Honey … he doesn't know where it is. You remember that night you helped me up the stairs?"

"Yes, Ma'am."

"Well, that night I was feelin' a little sickly … I was worried my time was near. I wrote you a note and wrapped it around the watch, then I put it in my windowsill. I was gonna give it to you the next mornin'" I looked at her rather puzzled. She grinned with a strange smile. "It's my secret spot were I hide things from yer Papaw and yer Daddy."

She leaned in close and whispered a secret. "Every woman has a secret hidin' spot like that." She winked with her index finger over her lips and I just smirked.

"Well … I put it in there and I went to sleep. The good Lord called me home that night and I didn't have a chance to give you the watch … You see?"

Again I was nodding.

" … Yer Daddy had no way of knowin' where it was."

I didn't know what to say … Just then, the lights on the bum leg went out. I could hear my Pap cursing under his breath. My Granny told him since his glasses were upstairs on the nightstand, that she would go down and change the fuse. She looked at me and then winked again.

"Honey, I'm so glad we could talk … I need you to remember that you and yer Daddy are all you got … you gotta look after one another … No matter what life a tosses ya."

"I know Granny, it's just so hard sometimes …"

"I know it is Dear, but you gotta take it as it comes … good *and* bad."

"You're right." I said.

"Well Honey, you have to run along and change that fuse now … "

My heart sank … I *knew* she'd be gone when I came back … I began to shake my head and pulled her in as close as I could.

Tears were streaming down my cheeks.

"No Granny … I don't want to leave you …"

She eased me back so that she could look into my eyes again.

"No Honey … you *never* leave me …" She put her palm on her chest.

" … Yer always right here … in my heart … You *and* yer Daddy"

I told her that she was in my heart too. She bit her lip and lovingly nodded.

"If anything Jefferson … I feel like *I left you* … *and* yer Daddy."

I was shaking my head as I spoke.

"No Granny … you didn't leave us … it was your time … that's life."

"You see?" Her face was beaming with pride again.

"You *do* understand." She pulled me in close for one last hug and kissed my forehead and my nose. "Now run along and change that fuse fer yer Papaw … and don't you go a forgittin' what I said … you and yer Daddy is all ya got …"

I kissed her cheek and turned to walk back to the basement. As I did, she began playing again …

When I got to the workbench I picked up the box of fuses and fished one out. I was wiping my tears on my sleeve as I sang one of my favorite songs along with her for one last time …

"This little light of mine … I'm gonna let it shine … Let it shine … Let it shine … Let it shine."

I screwed in the fuse and the basement was bright as all get out. I listened for the sound I knew I wouldn't hear. I sneezed at the pungent mildew and dust that filled the air. The wood chips under my boots crackled as I made my way to the stairs. I stepped into the entry hall and looked at the dingy carpet and doorknob. The wind was still blowing pretty hard outside, but the lights seemed to be holding steady.

I headed into the living room and stopped just past the archway. I stared at her organ. The cover was closed and her cane was leaning against the bench. I walked over and sat on it. I swore I could smell her … *Not her* perfume … Just *her*.

Closing my eyes, I listened to her words over and over again in my head. The fire was growing a little dim, so I went over and put another piece of wood on it, then I plopped on the couch and listened to the wind and the rain. The next thing I knew, it was morning; I was waking up to the rooster crowing and my Dad coming through the door …

I jumped up and ran to him. I threw my arms around him and squeezed with all my might.

"Well … it's good to see you too son … Surprised ya, did we?"

I let him go and looked up nodding.

"We couldn't find a motel with an open room nowhere … so we just drove all night through the storm and came on home." He said. I smiled at him and he slowly smiled back. I think he was a little surprised at my actions. I thought about my visit with my Granny … *and* how I was going to tell my Dad about it. I told him I missed him while he was gone and that I was real sorry for the way I'd been acting.

To my surprise, he told me that he was sorry too. Not often you heard those kinds of words from my Dad. I told him that Granny came to me in a dream and that she had told me where the watch was. He looked at me like I was crazy.

"You still asleep boy?"

I assured him that I wasn't and took his hand to lead him up the stairs to my Granny's room. When we walked in the room, we both went silent. The reverence that came over us as we looked around at her things wasn't measurable. Here … were all the earthly possessions of a person that meant so much to the both of us. The only thing I can compare it to is the feeling you get when you walk into a big empty church. The rich light from the rising sun just made it seem even holier. I squeezed his hand and silently led him over to the window. He was still looking at me like he thought I was asleep.

"Daddy, did you know that Granny hid things in her windowsill?"

"No, Son ... I didn't."

I reached down and began tugging and pulling every which way on the thin wooden sill. Suddenly, the front lifted up and there ... in a little hollow tray in the wall, was my Granny's little hiding spot. My Dad's eyes opened wide as we both looked down at the little wad of paper that sat in the middle of the tray. He looked down at me with a strange look on his face. "How did you find this, son?" I knew what he meant ... He thought I was snooping while he was gone.

"I didn't Dad ... I swear ... She told me in my dream where it was. She told me that we need to quit fighting and stick together 'cause we're all we got." I felt like I was lying, but he'd never believe that I'd actually *seen* her ... I wasn't totally sure that *I* believed it. He reached down in slow motion and picked up the paper. He bounced it lightly in his hand, feeling the weight. With his other hand, he opened the paper and the sun glinting off of its shiny gold casing hit us both in the eyes. He pulled it out of the paper and then read what she had written inside. He smiled as he did and then handed the watch to me.

"What's it say, Dad?" I asked him.

He looked at it again and then smiled at me as he read it out loud.

It said simply, "As promised. Love, Granny"

He folded the note and put it in his shirt pocket, then ruffled up my hair and told me that I'd better take really good care of the heirloom. He promised that he'd take real good care of the note.

I did take good care of that watch ... as a matter of fact, as of this writing, it's in my pocket keeping perfect time. I'm going to give it to my son this Christmas ... I just can't wait.

He has told me that he's wanted it ever since the day that I taught him how to tell time on it when he was just a little boy. I'd love to see him teach my grandson how to tell time on it. I fear sometimes in this day and age that tradition is becoming a lost practice.

Who knows, maybe I'll pass this story along to him as well.

My Dad and I never fought again ... well, not about anything that was of any consequence anyway.

He was called home by the Lord thirty-one years later in the spring of sixty-eight. A few years after that, I found the note tucked away in his old roll-top desk. It looked to me as though he had opened it up and refolded it many times through the years … We never really spoke too much of my experience after it happened. But, by the condition of the note, I'm pretty sure that he thought about it as often as I did.

Well, that's my story and I'm sticking to it. I have never forgotten about those precious moments that I shared with my Granny … Or the wisdom that she led me to on that windy fall evening.

The Power Company eventually found the source of our farms bum leg …

But … I have *never* found my wife's "Secret hidin' spot".

Jefferson Royal Robles

Sweet Silk Farms, Iowa

September 16th, 1978

I really loved writing this story. It is my favorite one from the "From Thee Edge" series. The only other time that I remember "enjoying" moments while writing a story was during several of the chapters in my first novel, "Wanderer". I don't mean that I don't enjoy the task of writing … I do … It's just that it's usually more of a focused, or even introspective feeling that I have when writing. If writing fiction, then I'm usually trying to keep the characters on track to blend the story elements all together to tell the tale at hand. I remember smiling several times as I wrote this story.

Being a Concert Production Electrician, the subject of electricity was a natural. But, the story came to me one day on the roof at 885 Park Ave. in Brooklyn. I was up there having some beers with the skyline (No, I didn't *always* cuss and swear at it!). It was cold … like low 40's and there had been snow on and off all week. This northern, NYC weather had brought on an ugly part of my geriatric onset … My knee was becoming really arthritic.

If it dropped below 50-ish, I had a bum leg. It made me visually limp.

I was up there with my parka on, drinking my flip-top Grolsch's and maybe smoking a bit. (Maybe). It was getting dark and I was watching the skyline do its color-changing performance. That's likely the reason I was braving the cold. I really did love it up there. It was my place of solace in the city. When you live there, you find one of those and you cherish it. Roof tops, in the boroughs especially, are simply the best. From any of these perches, you get that "million-dollar skyline view" the Realtor's love to pitch in search of more loot.

I was trying not to wince as my leg throbbed and the smell of the snow brought back a precious memory. It always does. You see, whenever I smell snow, I think of my Granny. We often went up from Florida to spend Christmas at her house in Pennsylvania and there was almost always snow. Even if it came a day or two after … that was still a 'White Christmas" for me. I've read that smell is the strongest trigger for memories. I guess I have to agree. When I smell that smell … I am back in her yard or on her porch … knowing the comfort that she is somewhere close by.

She was probably the most treasured person in my lifetime. My descriptions of the Granny character in this story are really me, speaking of her.

Her mannerisms and her "ways" … all *hers*.

In essence … you have now *met* my precious Granny. Even though my real granny didn't have one, mixing together the Granny in the story's bum leg and the bum leg of electricity was, as usual, my strange mind spinning a tale with the ingredients given at that moment … like frozen drinks in a blender.

Tequila?

Sure!

Lime Juice?

Absolutely!

How about Vodka, cranberry juice and grape juice?

Ohhhh, let's give *that* a whirl!

A Cran-Grape Siberian Slushy!

But, I digress ... (as usual).

 The other part ... the part not really spoken in the recipe ... is my missing her so deeply. Don't we all have *someone* like that in our lifetime? Well, I guess this was me missing her and somehow ... *bringing her back.*

Even if only on paper ...

 I think I just wanted to do what I had the protagonist do ... have *one more meeting* ... with her. In keeping with her memory and honoring her in the way she was so virtuous ... so caring ... so understanding ... I made her the hero.

 In my life, she *was* a Hero.

 All the descriptions of her quirks and even the psychology she that wielded so effortlessly ... those are *all* from my Granny. I bet she was somehow a likeness of one of your Grandmothers too. It also could have been your Mom, Aunt or even a neighbor from your childhood.

 Maybe not southern ... Maybe not with a limp ... But, I bet she had that loving ease that you loved to have put into you every time you were in her presence. If you've never had someone like this in your life, related to you by blood or not, then you have my sympathies ... as there is *no* feeling like that to be found *anywhere* else.

 Also, I hope that you can somehow glean that from my Granny character here. Especially if you didn't have one. The passion for this person is like no other ... and, I think I know why ...

 It's that unconditional love they relay to you so intensely. To be loved like that evokes an emotional response that we feel with few in our lives. It is very precious indeed.

 This person *loves you.*

 No ifs, ands ... or buts.

I swear, I'm not sure where the pocket watch came from. It just came as I wrote the story. I had to go back and add it to the opening of the story after it came. There is no metaphor intended there, not consciously on my part. Perhaps there is though ... a metaphor of precious time ... but I did not do that on purpose. That happens a lot. I knew when I began to write the story that I wanted to do the fuse thing. It was natural because it tied into the electricity thing. The same goes for the being on the farm part. My Granny lived in the country and was a Kentucky Hill woman, through and through. Of course, the bum leg bit was from *me* and my bum leg.

Now ... my Granny did *indeed* have a secret hiding spot in her window sill. That was something I wanted to have you relive with me as well. I had been sleeping in her big ol' steel-framed bed on a rainy day and when I opened my eyes, she was standing by the window and had it open, taking out her grocery money. I was amazed to see it was hidden there all along!

I asked her what she was doing ... and I'll never forget her shushing me with her finger over her lips. It was actually exciting ... I was sharing a secret with my precious Granny! She made me promise to keep that secret and I swore that I would ... and I did. She also told me that every woman has such a spot. That's where that whole element came from in the story. So help me ... the first time I'd *ever* spoken of it after that rainy morning, was when I wrote this story. Maybe it was fighting to get out of me, the same way my heart was burning to have just a few more precious moments with her.

I guess the protagonist is me, a bit. I was feisty and mischievous, like all other pre/early teen boys. I did have loving, but stern male figures, in my Father and Grandfathers, that I looked up to. I lost my Father at 6. I think that came through in the element of him losing his Mother and Grandfather. I guess I was relaying that feeling of loss I had experienced.

After reading this the first time, I was befuddled at the way the characters came alive and did what they did. They did follow *my pre-planned* storyline ... *mostly* ... but their *"elements"* of character and a few other nuances, like the whittling, the watch, and the whole corn farm part just happened. I knew he would see her again by putting the old fuse in the socket. I just didn't know quite how it would come to happen. The characters ... that live in my mind ... did that part all on their own. It happens to me all the time when I am writing fiction.

Honestly ...

It is my memories ... my experiences ... taking subliminal control of my hunting and pecking fingers as this story, and all other fiction that I've written so far, spilled out of me. I didn't even plan on it being told first person. But when I wrote the first line ... I saw what it was and just accepted it. In my humble opinion, it worked perfectly. The "bum leg" lesson was pre-planned. But *only* that. It was, obviously, the very heart of the idea for the story.

That and just him getting to see her one last time.

I also loved this lesson that she brought the protagonist. It really did make her the Hero, just like my Granny was to me. She had a way of smoothing over even the most deepest turmoil. She could dry tears faster than the Florida sun and bring smiles faster than a circus clown and she did it with that magic ingredient that seemed to be her very essence.

The essence of *every* Granny the world over ...

Love.

I hope you enjoyed that trip out to that old corn farm. I hope you enjoyed that little jaunt back into time ... I also hope that you enjoyed meeting my Granny. If she was alive ... I am certain that she would have enjoyed meeting you!

The Stop Sign On Gloucester Avenue

The sun lit up the inside of Stan Krychyk's eyelids like a bright red police beacon. He cursed his wife under his breath for opening the blinds. After all, she knew better. He hated to wake up to blinding light. But today, she was being particularly rude for one reason or another; he didn't really care. She hadn't performed her "wifely duties" in months; he wasn't worried about it though … after all … he had Erica for that.

He groaned the groan of an old tired dude as he rolled out of bed. Still keeping his eyes closed, he shuffled over to close the blinds; it was too early to pick up his feet when he walked. With a painful thud, he stubbed the middle toe on his left foot. It was the King Louie chair she'd bought at the auction the week before. "AH! SHIT!" he shouted hopping and dancing in pain around the room.

"The bitch probably left that monstrosity there on purpose!" He thought.

After closing the blinds, he plopped into the chair to inspect his foot. He looked like a pouting child with a fresh boo-boo. He pulled his lower lip back in as she walked in the room to see what all the commotion was about.

"What the hell are you doing up here Stanley?" She asked. "A Jig?"

"NO!" came the harsh reply of a spoiled brat who was having a bad day.

"I stubbed my toe on your piece of shit chair … "

He paused to massage it and his lip stuck back out instinctively, then he looked up at her with a scowl.

" … While I was trying to close the blinds that YOU left open!"

She rolled her eyes and reminded him that it was he, not her, who had opened the blinds last night before they went to sleep. She also backed up the defense with the fact that he had done so to point out to her that " … tomorrow we would have a full moon."

She breezed out the door shaking her head … it was pointless to argue with him.

Rebecca Krychyk's life was coming apart before her very eyes … How could this be? Stanley was such a great guy, he always had a smile and a kiss for her and he was usually up to some sneaky act of kindness.

He loved to see the look of surprise on her face when he brought her flowers or a present.

At least that's what he had always told her …

At least that's what she liked to remember …

Now, it seemed … he didn't have a heart at all.

Rebecca fought back a tear as she arranged the flowers in the huge, hand-painted vase on the landing of the staircase. The kids wiped them out, without fail, every morning on their way downstairs to breakfast and she wouldn't want him to see a bad flower arrangement. She had loved him since childhood in their small neighborhood across town. That seemed like light-years ago and ever since he had bought this old mansion, she'd never felt like things were the same. She couldn't figure out if it was the fame and fortune, or the removal of himself from his old surroundings but, something had changed in him for sure … and it was not good.

She hurried the children along with their breakfast and noticed with motherly concern that both hadn't said much this morning. In fact, they hadn't even fought amongst themselves, a sure sign "Somthin' was a-brewin'".

Stan ambled down the stairs and bumped the flower arrangement in the huge hand-painted vase on the landing of the stairs. He brushed and inspected his sweater for foliage remnants as he mumbled something about her putting that there on purpose too. He slowed as he passed the fish tank and tried to see if this Beta was the new one or the old one. He hadn't had time to finish watching the "Battle Royal", as he liked to call it; He had to get upstairs and catch his nightly call from Erica.

It seemed the new blue Beta he brought home last night was giving the old one a run for his money.

"How stupid to put such a small "feminine" fish in such a large tank. 'Becca had to be out of her mind". He thought.

Stan fought the idea tooth and nail right up until she explained what kind of fish it was …

"Rumble Fish, Huh?" was his response.

From that day forward, his evil game of dropping in opponents in her absence was one of his greatest delights. "She's so stupid, she's never even noticed! "He thought to himself as he started to limp his way into the kitchen. When he saw that no one was paying attention, he let out a suppressed "oooh, aaaaah" in sync with his over-dramatized limp.

"You okay Stanley?" Rebecca inquired.

"You KNOW I'm not! … I think I broke a couple of toes on that damned chair! I can hardly walk!"

The children got up in unison and headed for the garage door. "

We'll be waiting in the car for you Daddy." Angelica said in a somber, little tone that showed her fear for her dad's apparent mood. Her eyes never met his. Little Stan was even quieter as he spoke on his way out the door, "I hope your foot gets better Daddy."

"Damn it 'Becca!" He spewed slapping his hand on the table. "I've got to take them again?"

She spun around with a fire in her eye and proceeded to give him a full two-minute piece of her mind. Meanwhile, he rubbed the sting from his tender hand. "Stanley Archibald Krychyk!" she began ... He didn't hear much of the next part as he drifted off into a daydream about how much he hated his name ... And he hated it when she reminded him he had the same middle name as his great grandpa ... he hated the whole name.

He remembered all the bullies in grade and middle school who made fun of him constantly ...

"Sad Sack!"(A takeoff on his initials)

"Archie-Fartchie!'

"Staaaan-lee!" ...

He'd heard them all ... and he heard them a lot.

Why did his Great Grandpa have to have such a geeky name?

Why did his dad have to give him such a curse?

He so much preferred his pen name ... Stan Priest.

It had such a nice ring to it ... Romantic ... mysterious ... it fit him he thought ... But just then, her lecture came back into focus when she stepped in front of his face and asked if he'd heard a word that she had said.

"How could I not?" he shot back at her ... "The friggen' fish in the pond up the road could hear YOU yellin'!" She started to say something else, but he cut her off ...

"Can't you just be nice to me in the morning?" he pleaded.

"Nice?" she interjected. "You mean like getting our kids up, dressed and fed while you sleep?"

He opened his mouth but she was already speaking again.

"Not to mention the fact that I do this after you shut the alarm off instead of hitting the snooze bar … By the time I wake up, I'm running late for work!"

He knew what was coming next … You learn these things when you get into the same fight over and over again. He stood up and began to shout while he lightly tapped his palm with the back of his other hand. "We've been through this time and again 'Becca, if we put the alarm on your side of the bed and you're not there to shut it off, then I have to roll all the way to your side of the bed to get to it … and I HATE that!"

But she had also been in the same ring with the same opponent many times before, and she wasn't going to let him off that easy.

"Well if I didn't have to drive an hour and a half to work every day … EACH WAY …!"

"Here it comes again." he thought … Her words came off in a cadence like she'd said them a thousand times before … She had.

"I still can't believe that I worked so hard to make my decorating business a success to put you through college!" She pleaded.

He interjected to the best of his ability …"And I told you I'd pay you back one day, didn't I?"

She blew up at his statement because he made her lose her train of thought and then, in frustration, she began to scream …"MY FAMILY! YOUR FAMILY! … MOST OF OUR FRIENDS!… "

This was the part he hated most … "They all told me your writing career would never amount to anything!" The veins in her forehead were bulging out a little more with each word.

"Did I listen? … NO!!

I believe in you I said …

He's gonna be wonderful I said …

EIGHT YEARS LATER …

Eight YEARS later …YOU GET A BREAK!

And was it some grand novel that'll be turned into a movie?

Was it a literary masterpiece reveled by scholars the world over?

Or was it even an award-winning children's story?

OF COURSE NOT!

NOOOOOO, my husband writes trashy dime store novels that he's so ashamed of, he had to CHANGE HIS NAME to do it!"

This is where she usually took a breath and he dove on the opportunity to try and save himself ... "You know those agent people made me do that ... "

He gave his most pitiful sad look ...

"They said no one would buy a book from "STANLEY ARCHIBALD Krychyk!" He looked pitiful.

"I hate using an alias and you know it, sweetums!" ... He was doing his best to act like the old Stan but she just wasn't buying it today.

"So is this the part where you try and tell me you bought me this house as repayment for my efforts?"

She paced around the kitchen and wrung her hands as she struggled for the perfect and yet new line that might make him see her side of things.

"I didn't want this house and you didn't hear a word I said that day you called from the bank." She stopped pacing and stared straight at him ... she felt she might be on to something.

"You wanted this house just so you could take that stupid road to and from town ... Couldn't you have found another road ... on OUR side of town? "If she was on to something, she lost it ... She was out of breath and felt overwhelmed with futility as she spun around to hide the tears welling up in her eyes.

Never one to miss a shot at a downed opponent, Stan came back full force with, "swee'pee ... You know I write my best stuff on that romantic old road ... I wrote my first best-selling piece on that road!"

She took one last shot at him just to make him hurt a little ...

"Piece?

PIECE?

"Fields of Sin?"

"You call *that* ... a *piece*?"

She laughed as mean as she could, then finished her attack with; "Oh, it's a piece alright ... A piece in the hayloft ... a piece in the basement ... a piece in the cab of a combine ... a piece in the old church house for crying out loud!"

She was so exasperated; she was losing her breath. Her words got farther and farther apart as she finished her brutally truthful attack ...

"You took a bunch of your perverted sexual fantasies and you put them to work on a farm!

You took six years of schooling and you tied all the characters together with a really cheesy storyline that let them have sex every four pages!"

She had said so much, that she wondered for a moment if he had tuned her out as he did so often. He said nothing and she didn't give him one moment to do so either …

"A seventeen-year-old with his hormones all a raging could write that drivel!" She screamed, palms up, "When are you going to make me proud and write something we can show our families?" She pleaded.

Stan had heard enough … he turned without saying a word and went out the garage door …

How could she not appreciate what she had? He thought. Why was it so bad to make his money this way? She had everything she needed. Big deal she had a great business … couldn't she think of him for one minute?

He loved that road … it let his mind wander. When he talked his first sleazy story into the minidisc recorder that she had bought him for their anniversary, he was on that road. That road let his mind wander just far enough from reality to let his creative juices flow. Big deal they were dime store novels …

He had made over three million dollars on selling only five manuscripts. A good agent, four or five scripted, risqué' radio interviews and VOILA! Instant best-selling author! So what if he spent almost two million on buying and fixing up this old place. It wasn't his money … it was her income for the down payment and the rest he borrowed with the property as collateral. He could sell the back half of the property for that matter. The kids didn't need all that room to play anyway … besides, it would be a lot less wear and tear on his new riding lawnmower … *and* less time that *he* had to spend riding it. If he sold just a few more manuscripts, he could stop writing such fluff and get on to his biggest piece yet …

Or not … Perhaps he would just grab Erica, drain most of the savings account and head down to Costa Rica or Jamaica maybe.

Hell, with that kind of money … why would he be worried about pleasing the wifey anyway? Okay, so he hadn't sold a 'script in two and a half years … the old bags and trailer trash were bound to buy his next one, he dreamed.

As they rolled up Gloucester Avenue, the tires of the shiny new Caddy hissed over the wet blacktop … They sounded like sizzling bacon to little Stan. "We sure have been getting a lot of rain, haven't we Dad?" His timid voice was lost in the cavernous backseat. Stan wouldn't have heard him anyway. He was checking his voicemail on the cell phone. He wanted to hear when he was going to meet with Erica tonight. He wanted to hear from his agent that he had sold again. He wanted to hear from his secretary that a royalty check had arrived at his office. Anybody that would bring him good news or cheer and make him forget about the morning he was having.

The only message there though was from his old grade-school pal Roy on the county commission.

He never really cared for Roy … but, he was the ticket for Stan's latest pet project and he was calling to confirm their breakfast appointment for nine-thirty. Stan looked at his watch and then shook his head and sighed as he California-stopped at the sign he hated so much.

A small smirk crept across his lips as he stared at the stop sign in disdain.

"All in good time my little pretty … All in good time. "He thought.

Stan winced at the splash of muddy water that covered the hood and windshield as he drove through the puddle in front of Angelica's school. "Ahhh, Christ!" He said under his breath.

"When I come home tonight I want you two to wash Daddy's car inside and out, you hear?" There was a long silence in the car as the siblings pondered the last three-hour car detailing fiasco. Their father was *never* completely satisfied … *ever*.

"Do we get twice the allowance for doing it twice in one week Daddy?" Angelica said in her best little angel voice. For her appearance, her name fit her like a glove. But Angelica Krychyk was approaching that age where you begin to see through the smokescreen adults confuse children with all too often.

When his reply came back as a command that they will do what he says, WHEN he says it, she turned her eyes out the window and thought of her Mom.

Angelica took a deep, hopeful breath and began the plea she had practiced the entire evening before …

Dad, I need some money to get a prom dress … It's coming up in two weeks and if I don't go, I'll feel like the biggest loser in the school."

He turned to her impatiently and retorted "There's a "help wanted" sign on the door to Sallie's diner, why don't you go fill out an application and see if you can get a job there after school or on weekends? You know, nobody ever handed me anything when I was your age."

She started to reply but she was afraid he would see her crying. He had no patience for tears … and he usually only got madder at the first sign of them.

"Thanks for the ride Dad." was all she said, closing the door and running into her school as the rain, like her tiny tears of frustration began to fall hard and fast.

Stan looked across the street at his son's school and then let out a long impatient sigh as he looked back at little Stan. "I guess you want me to drive you over there … besides if you caught a cold your Mom would kill me in my sleep!" After checking his watch once again, Stan muddled the Caddy through the traffic jam of school buses and doting parents. When he realized that the drive around the circle to the drop-off point would take a while, he turned to him in the rear-view and said in his most convincing voice …

"I think the rain let up son, you think you could make it up there without getting TOO wet?"

The little guy could barely make out the front of the school through the rain. He shivered at the thought of running through it. He tried to prolong his warm dry ride with a question of his own.

"Dad, you remember you said I could play football?"

He didn't wait for a reply and he followed right through with the meat of his query.

"They told us in gym class yesterday that if we want to play football in Angelica's school next year that we have to go to summer football camp starting the second week of vacation. I was hoping …"

Stan looked at his watch and shook his head, interrupting the boy.

"Can you get to the point there kiddo, I've got an important meeting to get to."

The young boy's hopes fell into the pit of his stomach as he uttered the punch line he too had practiced all morning in his head to deliver. He felt defeated even before he spoke …

"I need a hundred and nineteen dollars for tuition, insurance, and equipment … If I don't go to the …" Stan's voice rattled the vents in the car as he proceeded to explain to the boy how much he'd paid in taxes last year and how THAT should pay for his gear to play football. He said that they could discuss it later, but the little man knew it would never happen. No one could play the "I'm busy right now, Son" game, like his dad. He opened the door without warning and made a beeline for the front of his school.

Stan looked puzzled yet relieved as he watched his son run towards the school and vanish in the deluge that was now blanketing the schoolyards like a fog. He turned onto the main drag and headed for Sallie's.

All the parking spaces that were anywhere close to the diner's awning were

L

taken. Stan cursed under his breath and looked at his watch again … "Shit-nine-forty! … If he's not in here I'm gonna scream! … I waited three weeks for this meeting!" Stan paused and shook his head with his eyes closed …

"If I missed him because of those snotty-nosed little brats I'm gonna kill someone!"

He whipped the car into a handicap space right up front and hopped out of the car like the rain was going to make him melt. As he walked through the door, the first thing he noticed was the absence of his favorite little hostess … Erica.

He scanned the whole room, then the hallway leading to the restrooms. His shoulders fell as he exhaled in disappointment … She was nowhere to be seen.

"Ah well, maybe that's why she hadn't called yet …" He thought. " … She probably stayed home sick."

Sallie took a look at Stan and snatched up the cordless phone as she went behind the counter and disappeared into the kitchen.

The diner seemed awfully busy for such a dreary day and the smell of bacon grease and coffee filled the air. Roy waved his arms frantically and Stan forgot about Erica as his other major motive kicked into play.

"Well, HEY there Roy ole buddy, how's the wife and kids?" His voice couldn't have been more plastic if Tupperware had made it.

Roy Justice was a strapping big man, a farming man, and he looked a little uncomfortable in his dark blue store-bought suit. He fidgeted with the tight collar almost constantly. The bright red tie was just a little too thin for a man of his girth. It looked like it had been tightened and loosened far too many times today.

"Well, I've spoken to my colleagues on the council and we're pretty sure we can make this thing happen for you there, Stan." He spoke while he shoveled another forkful of biscuits and gravy into his mouth.

"Pretty sure? … What do you mean … Pretty sure?" Stan snapped, as he motioned the already busy Sallie to his still empty coffee cup.

"You said if I took care of you, you would take care of me … didn't you?"

Roy swallowed a big gulp of coffee to wash down his B&G and then held out his coffee cup to Sallie just as she got to the table. Stan looked at him like a greedy kid who just watched the bully get the last piece of apple pie. Sallie then turned, filled Stan's cup and asked if he'd like his usual.

"Not today baby, but your phone number would be nice."

Stan's grin was as perverse as his tone of voice. She left the table without wasting her breath on a reply.

Roy set his fork down and grabbed five packs of sugar from the bowl. He stacked them up in his hand and tore them open all at once. As he poured them into his cup, he began to speak again.

"Well now you know Stan, changing stop signs and whatnot takes city planners and traffic engineers and then there's the …" Stan's morning had gone bad enough. This was not what he wanted to hear."

Roy, can you do it or not?" He interrupted; it almost killed him not to shout.

"Like I said, if you hold up your end of the bargain; I don't see any problems. BUT … " He stared up at Stan." … You know how politics go … nothing's guaranteed."

Stan reached in his coat pocket and retrieved the five crisp, new hundred-dollar bills that he had withdrawn from the bank the day before. He placed them neatly in the menu and slid it across the table. Roy, still chewing his next bite of B&G, nodded his head while he placed the bills in the inside pocket of his jacket.

"Tell me something, Stan." He asked, "Why is it so imperative that you get this sign swapped around?"

Stan reached out with a mischievous grin grabbing Sallie's leg. She slapped his hand and threw the bill on the table. She motioned like she was going to pour hot coffee on him and then turned away to another table.

Stan picked up the check and looked at Roy; this time like a guy who'd just won the football pool. "I do my best writing on that road. You just wouldn't believe how many storylines I've lost pulling up to that stop sign. It breaks my concentration. Now imagine the stories your wife could read if I didn't have that stupid thing there, you know? … Besides, Gloucester is just over ten miles long … And Winston Street is less than a mile … Why make someone on the LONG road stop?"

Roy shook his head in amazed agreement and then asked Stan if he'd remembered the other part of their deal …

He hadn't … until now.

"I'll tell you what, the day they switch the stop sign, I'll be out to your house with an entire set of my books for your wife." Roy cocked his head to remind Stan that he was still forgetting something …

"And, of course, they'll all be autographed."

Roy stood up grinning and shook Stan's hand, then started to dig in his pockets.

"Oh no, my friend, this ones on me," Stan said, as he waived his platinum Visa around in the air.

"Well, let me get the tip then." Roy said, still rummaging around in his pockets.

"I wouldn't hear of it big guy."

Stan gazed out through the diner windows …

"Now, the rain has stopped; why don't you head on out before it starts up again?" Roy nodded and headed for the door. Stan turned and threw eight singles down for a $7.44 bill.

His only thought was "How could Roy eat so much?"

Stan felt his day go from bad to good to worse when he saw the ticket on his windshield.

"AWWW CHRIST! Can you BELIEVE this? We don't even HAVE handicaps in this back-ass country town!" He looked back at Sallie just in time to see an evil grin leave her face. He scraped up the soggy ticket and threw it on the passenger's seat, then peeled out as he left the diner parking lot.

His mind was brewing up a way to get even with Pete the cop for picking on him.

"Well, I only have two more fires to put out and I'm outta here for the day!" He thought out loud to himself as he turned down the alleyway behind his offices. He always parked back here because it was less of a walk than from the parking garage. He looked down the alley and saw a bag lady scrounging around a dumpster. Suddenly, he had a flash for his next piece … "Lust in the alley".

"Not bad. Not bad" He thought. In the elevator, he flailed his arms like he was having convulsions … His face in a tight grimace like he'd just won the grand prize … "I can write in this down and out actress/model who shows the bums that they can get some lovin' too!"

His ego was feeling rather inflated as he blew into his office like a storm. His thick, perverse wind swirling around his latest secretary.

Heather was a sweet looking blonde that Stan had hired in a bar on her looks alone.

Who cared about her office skills if he could get in her pants? But, that day had not come in weeks and, like the last poor girl he had hired, then fired; he had given her the ultimatum … put out or get out.

She looked at him nervously from her chair and told him, in her best professional voice, that he had three messages. He took the messages and grabbed her hand rather firmly.

He pulled her face close to his and reminded her of the talk they had yesterday and how she had better make up her mind by the end of the week …

He let her go and she turned her eyes away from him and began to type.

Neither one noticed that there wasn't any paper in the typewriter …

Stan sauntered off to his office whistling a strange, eerily happy tune. He was looking over his messages as he walked …

Rebecca, ten A.M … He tossed it on the floor …

His agent, ten-twenty A.M … He tossed it on the floor as well …

ERICA!

That was what he was hoping for! Maybe this day would brighten up after all. The message read simply: "Sorry I missed you at breakfast. My car wouldn't start this morning. Please call me." Stan plopped into his high-backed, winged, leather office chair and began to spin around in it like a child on an amusement ride. He stopped spinning only when he noticed he hadn't closed the door all the way. He jumped up and kicked the door shut. He danced over and hit the speed dial on the cordless as he returned to his desk.

"Hello?" Came the breathy voice of the young redhead on the other end of the phone.

"Hi, my little lovin's!" Stan spouted in his best baby voice. "Did your car go broke-broke?"

There was a short silence on the other end, and then she came back with the same type of baby voice … "Yes, and I'm very saaaad … It made me miss my wookwooks … Will you come get me so we can play? I suuuuuure miss my wookywook."

She purred like a cat for about ten seconds and Stan started to come unglued.

"I miss you a whole lot too, my babes … Would you like to go out for some din-din a little later? "Sorry." Came the reply "My Mumsie's already making me din-din … But I'm going to have YOU … for deeee-zert!" Her statement ended in an evil, knowing laugh.

The mention of her mother reminded Stan of her age … Twenty-one … Half his age. He had met her at the diner and she was so enthralled by his writings … They were, it seemed, her first encounter with erotica and she flirtatiously told him how sexually talented the author of such steamy stories must be. In less than three hours he had her at the small motel on the west side of town.

She was too inexperienced to notice just how untalented he really was.

He ... could care less ...

They agreed to meet at the old railroad yard just around the corner from her house.

He was already trying to think of an angle to get in her pants before they went to the drive-in. She would never put out there anyway, he thought. She was scared someone would catch them and they had had that discussion many times before.

"I'm gonna go home to get all fresh for my baby-cakes and then I'll see you at the rail yard at say ... 7:45?" This would give him more than an hour to get some pre-movie action. "Ooooo ..." She came back all breathy again. " ... It's all so ... so ... cloak and dagger ... God this makes me so hot ..."

Stan heard his door squeak and looked up to see his agent standing in the doorway ... He hadn't heard him knock ... twice.

"Hun, I've got an important meeting to attend to ... I'll call you back ... " He hung up without hearing her say goodbye.

"And to what do I owe this pleasure, Mr. Cook?"

"Save it for the chickies Stan-o, this is business."

He stared at the floor as he almost cautiously made his way over to the small plastic chair in front of Stan's desk. He hated coming here. He had met with Stan many times before ... He didn't like his writing ... or him.

"Listen," He continued, " ... The publishing house is telling me that they are going to have to drop us if you don't deliver some sell-able product here soon."

He sounded like a dad trying to explain to a child why they were selling his puppies.

Stan spent the rest of his morning telling the agent about the new story he had written and how he could read it just as soon as he proofed it. The agent didn't feel any better as he left the office ...

But then, he never felt good in the presence of Stan Krychyk anyway.

Stan looked at his watch and calculated that he needed to leave now if he wanted to:

Get home ...

Have the kids clean the car ...

Eat his dinner ...

Get a shower and get out to the rail-yard in time …

In time to maul her before the movie.

"There's a call for you on line three." The voice on his intercom almost made him jump out of his skin. "MMMM, line three huh?" He knew who that was.

He only gave that number to little hotties and since he had no other irons in the fire …

It must be ERICA!

"How come you didn't call me back, pumpkin? I've been missing my James Bond all day …"

"Me too, my little Mata Hari … And when I get my hands on you … Ooooo there's gonna be fire in the sky! But I still have some fires to put out … 7:45 … right?"

"I'm counting the minutes!" She replied.

"I'm gonna go now! Kisses!" She couldn't hear his pathetic insincerity. Stan thought he heard her say "Kisses!" as he hung up the phone. He sighed and bolted out the door.

He cupped Heather's breasts from behind in one firm single motion, holding them so tight it almost hurt. Then he bit her right ear as he reminded her through his teeth that she had two more days to decide how things were going to be around here …

She tensed up as hard as a board and didn't say a word. She was frozen in fear. Her skin was crawling …

He bopped out of the office smelling her perfume on his chin, thinking how sweet it was going to be when he finally had his way with her … The dream flashed in his twisted thoughts all the way down to the alley. He picked up the mini-disc recorder and plugged it into the lighter socket as he began to steer the Caddy towards Gloucester Avenue.

Stan set the cruise control and began to ramble his new story onto the mini-disc. This one would have to be built fast … His agent's ultimatum echoed in his head. He started babbling the story by having the main character, "Heather" getting nailed by a movie producer on a casting couch …

"When she reads that I used her name in one of my books, she'll be so flattered, there's no way she'll resist me then." He thought to himself. An evil grin was beaming across his face.

Stan stared down Gloucester Avenue and kept rambling his twisted smut like a kid enjoying his favorite song. The road was almost perfectly straight and surrounded by the most beautiful rolling farm and pastureland this country has ever tossed up. He could see the stop sign in the distance and almost lost his place when he concentrated on it a little too long.

He rambled a segue of the young actresses descent from rising star to street bum and couldn't believe what was about to happen …

He stabbed the brakes and cursed a slew of epithets at the old woman in the full-size pick-up truck.

"Damn you, you old bag!" He shouted. "Why don't you watch where you're driving?"

It wasn't her fault … He had done one of his infamous California rolling stops … She was just driving along on a through street, minding her own business … Stan didn't notice that she had to pull over to regain her composure …

His concern now was that when he played back his disc-recorder to the voice recognition on his computer, he would have to stop both machines to edit out his tongue lashing of the elderly driver.

He rambled on and on all the way to his driveway. As he turned off the mini-disc, he had more lurid thoughts about his meeting with Erica this evening … That would be just what he needed … to inspire the rest of his new seedy tale.

When Stan opened the garage door and limped into the kitchen, Having turned it on like a switch, he looked around and began to huff and puff … He was looking around for someone to coddle him … his lower lip protruding like a thorn.

Something wasn't right …

He couldn't quite pinpoint it.

But … one thing was for sure … he was alone.

With his hands on his hips and a stomp of his left foot, he cursed out his displeasure at the empty house.

"She must have taken the little terrors to their Gramma's house for dinner." He saw the LED flashing on the answering machine but there was no time. He had to hurry if he was going to have enough time to shower and get back to the all-night car wash before his tryst with the Redhead.

"DAMN IT BECCA!" he thought, "COULDN'T YOU JIVE WITH MY PLANS … JUST ONCE?"

He could wave some hot dogs for dinner, but the car wash was going to push his time envelope to the limit. He bounded up the stairs two at a time. At the top of the stairs, Stan noticed that his computer had been left on all day ... He had left it on after checking his e-mail.

"Damn those brats!" He cursed, "I swear to God, I'm uninstalling those stupid games TOMORROW!"

He continued huffing, "Computers are for work and if they think they have time to play games then they're in for quite a shock when they see next week's chore list! I've told them a thousand times to shut this thing off when they're through!"

He simmered down only long enough to fire up the voice recognition program and start it to recording what he'd "written" on the way home.

He returned to his grumblings as he hopped into the shower. Again ... he felt something strange as he showered, but he still couldn't quite pinpoint it. No matter how he twisted and writhed under the stream of the shower ... he didn't feel clean ...

It was strange ... like the water didn't feel right ... Even when he opened his mouth and filled it, then spit it back out ... It didn't taste right. It was dry and when it hit his tongue, instead of feeling soft and warm, it felt like stinging little pinpricks. The sound of the water on the tile and granite floor was muffled ... like he had water in his ears. The seemingly deadening of his senses made him realize that it was an instinct he was never aware of before. For a moment he felt like he wasn't alone ...

Or maybe that he was *too* alone ...

He quit thinking about it and turned off the shower.

Stan mimed his own words as he listened to the playback of the disc. He hurriedly toweled off and began to vigorously dry his now-balding head with a different towel.

He sat on the edge of his desk, hovering over the player as the moment of the cursing approached ...

He stared at the recorder as the sound of skidding tires filled the room ...

In shock, he listened to the sound of himself saying; "Oh my God ... NOOOOOO!"

The unmistakable terror in his voice was all too real ...

His shriek was instantly followed by a tremendous, booming CRUNCH.

The sound of breaking glass and twisting metal was finally silenced by the sound of escaping steam ...

And silence.

"WHAT IN THEE HELL IS GOIN' ON AROUND HERE TODAY? He screamed.

He fast-forwarded ... and soon found the sound of approaching sirens ...

Listening in terror, he heard the ambulance drivers footsteps get closer to the microphone.

"Hey Phil, ya think we can get him out?

"Naaah," Came the reply, " ... there's no need just yet, I checked his vitals ... I doubt he felt a thing."

There was a moment of silence and then the other voice spoke ... send chills down Stan's spine ...

"Yeah, this one too ..." Stan could hear more steps on the broken glass ... "She looks like she didn't have much time left anyhow ... What a shame."

There was a long pause and then, as the sound of steam started to dwindle, he heard the two voices discussing how well the Caddy had held up to the impact with the large white pick-up truck.

Stan's heart was in his throat and his breaths were getting shorter and shorter. The beads of moisture were not from his shower but from the sweat that was accompanying the panic attack he knew was about to hit him like a baseball bat. "What is happening to me?" He thought. "Am I dreaming?"

He looked at his shaking hand as he began to hear the sound of an approaching siren again.

One of the ambulance drivers was saying something ...

But all Stan could make out was "Maybe Pete could tell us what happened here."

His partner's reply came across somewhat sarcastic "What are you kiddin' me? He ran the stop sign! It doesn't take a rocket scientist to figure that one out ... JEEEEZ!"

There was a moment of silence then the other guy came back with ... "Yeah, but why?"

By this time, the approaching siren had stopped and Stan could hear the sound of a slamming car door, then the sound of Pete the cop's voice calling in a tow truck.

"Wotcha got fellas?" He inquired ...

"Well we're gonna need the coroner for both I'm afraid." Was the only reply.

The sound of footsteps on broken glass was all he could hear for about thirty seconds. He winced with every crunch ...

He strained to hear every sound on the disk ... He thought it odd that the sound wasn't muffled as it had been in the shower. Then, Stan heard Pete calling for the coroner on his radio ...

"That's right John ... TWO body bags!"

The words and sounds echoed in Stan's head like an approaching clap of thunder.

"How can this be real?"

"How can this be happening?"

He felt the panic well up inside his chest and he got up to look around for some shred of sanity. Then he thought about Erica ...

A sly grin crossed his lips and for a few moments, he let his anguish go. Then, just as he took his first easy breath, he heard the sounds of someone fumbling around with the recorder ...

"W'addia got there Petey?" Said the first paramedic.

"It's a voice recorder ... this one is that writer from up the road here ... He bought the old Levy mansion.

"Sorry ... I thought you knew who he was." There was some discussion on the merits of his writings and then Pete's last words made Stan's blood run cold ...

"Ah, no great loss anyway ... The guy was a jerk to my wife, Sallie, at the diner all the time ... and a lousy tipper too. The way I see it, if he'd paid more attention to the road and not work, he'd probably be home by now ... Well, I guess he won't be needing this anymore."

There was a soft pop on the disc ... and then silence.

Stan fast-forwarded through the rest of the disc; desperately seeking the rest of what he had "written" ...

Nothing ... but dead air.

In a panic, he threw the recorder into the wall with a crash ... Pieces went flying in every direction. He grabbed a handful of hair with each fist and looked at the pieces strewn around the room like trash in the stands after a hockey game. He took a few deep breaths, but he could not stop the frightening confusion that was slowly overtaking him.

He looked at the clock … "7:02?! … SHIT!" Desperate … He tried to go back to his plans.

"Well, I better let the mutt out since no one else is here to do it."

He was trying to ignore what was going through his head. He ran downstairs, relishing in the moment that he was able to let go of what he had just heard. The thought of Erica spread across his front seat was a reality break he needed very desperately.

As he passed the huge hand-painted vase at the landing of the stairs, he noticed that the flower arrangement was gone …

"Isn't that strange … "

It was a statement … *not* a question …

As he really didn't care if 'Becca took the flowers to work or what … it just SEEMED strange.

He called out to the dog, but got no response …

He searched the whole house and decided that the dog must already be in the backyard.

When he opened the French double doors in the back of the house … He noticed something almost immediately … There was no wind. The weather fronts that had been moving through the area for the last few hours were blowing up a storm, " … not minutes ago." He thought.

He looked around for, and called out to, the dog. But still, he got no response. It wasn't until he had gotten back up on the porch that he had his second jolt of weirdness …

He couldn't hear any birds …

Or crickets …

Or planes … In fact, in all his life, he had never experienced such total and utter silence …

He looked up and was suddenly covered in goosebumps … There wasn't a cloud in the sky!

Stan ran back in the house and tried to collect himself.

His head was beginning to throb as he bolted for the front door.

"That stupid mutt probably dug another hole under the fence!" he whined, " … And if they think I'm gonna bail him out of the pound again, they're nuts!"

He was trying to not think about the last few minutes of his life when he noticed something else that made him feel one step closer to panic.

There were no fish in the fish tank … not dead … not alive … no fish at all!

He ran to the Rumble Fish bowl … it was empty.

He wiped the sweat from his face and glanced around the room … Turning pale as he noticed that ALL the flowers … ALL the family photos … Were GONE!

"Did she up and leave me?" He screamed as he squeezed his head tight from the pain.

That was almost what he hoped for as he began to reason with just what was happening to him. "But why would she take the flowers?" He thought to himself. He opened the front door and again experienced the same strange and eerie calm of the backyard … He called out … but still no dog.

As he was about to close the door in silence, he noticed his car was gone from the driveway … Another jolt of reality. As much as he loved that car, it was a welcome sight … He could call the Police and they would bring him back to the real world. Slamming the door, he dashed towards the phone.

He felt almost comforted. He fumbled for the numbers and stared out the front picture window hoping to see his wife … his kids … his neighbor … the mutt … ANYONE coming up the drive.

He had just about drifted into one of his trances when he heard a woman say something on the other end of the line about being the Police Department and asking what she could do for him …

He didn't listen; he just blurted out before she could finish; "Yes … I'd like to report a stolen car … !"

There were a few moments of silence …

And then she replied; "I'm sorry Mr. Krychyk … We don't have cars here …"

He held the phone in front of his face and yelled angrily; "But, how did you know my name!?" He paused for a moment … holding the phone out in front of his face. For the first time since he could remember, he felt tears in his eyes. He had forgotten what they felt like. He blinked them away and stared at the receiver.

His hand was shaking uncontrollably.

He shouted at the phone … "I didn't tell you my name!"

He stared at it … like it was someone he was about to fight … Then all the expression left his face. He looked all around him … *nothing* was right.

He slowly opened his hand and the phone slid out and fell with a thump on the new Berber carpet. He walked back towards the front door, slowly … *knowingly* … nodding his head. The conversation on the voice recorder replaying in his head …

A strange calm overtook him as he began to accept this new reality.

The handle was now searing hot as he closed his eyes and opened it …

He didn't need to look …

He knew what was before him … the dry, searing heat was already taking his breath away and burning his skin …

The tears that had begun to well from his eyes were gone immediately … he could feel them dry on his cheeks …

Stanley Archibald Krychyk took his first steps into Hell … and gently closed the door behind him.

This story is the first instance where I had ever manipulated fictional characters on paper. I'm rather fond of it for that reason. I had the idea come to me while looking into ways to "talk not type", as I still hunt and peck!

Absurd, I know. But my fingers are just too big and fumbley to actually type all proper-like. I would spend more time fixing typos! I can actually blaze near 50 words a minute when focused and I do use more than two fingers sometimes ... so speed makes up for technique in my case. I was hoping to find the gear and software to write without typing ... *too* much.

Go ahead and laugh, dear Reader ... it's all good.

It's not that I'm lazy. My issue is my life-long ADHD. They used to call it simply:

"Hyperactive".

I preferred that.

I'm impatient when it comes to my own output. I can drive myself way too hard sometimes. (And I'm guessing some who have worked with me will say that I can do the same to them. Mea Culpa). Well ... It took me 2 YEARS to write my first novel. But ... I stopped for nearly 7 months with writer's block and being too busy/tired to write. I had just begun to write fiction stories, I just wanted to speed up the process.

While I was looking into speech-to-text software and portable voice recorders, I also at that period in my life, had a friend that was just absolutely selfish. As I got to know him better, I couldn't believe how manipulative he actually was with everybody in his life!

I watched him operate as we hung out and it seemed that everyone that I watched him interact with within his day was some kind of "tool" in his world, for lack of a better way to put it. No matter who we encountered, he was getting something from them. I was awestruck at this realization.

It also made me realize that I was one of them! He was so good at passive-aggressive, that he could quite often get folks to do his bidding while feeling like they owed him the favor (they did not) or, before they realized it, that he had tricked them into doing it as if they were doing him a favor! In a weird way, it was fascinating to watch him work, seeing as how I love to study people in general.

I'd known him since Junior High. But, we didn't begin hanging out until in our 30's. Not being born yesterday ... after a few of these manipulations being done to me, I confronted him on the next one. In a typical, predictable sociopath response, he said something like "Fine" and tore off in his truck like

I was supposed to feel bad and maybe call him back and do what he was asking.

I didn't.

After a few days, again, in typical predictable sociopath behavior ... he rang me up, acted as if nothing happened ... and began setting me up for the next manipulation!

SO amazing!

Trying a different angle with me, he first gave me a really nice gift. It was his way of making up for ticking me off earlier ... or so it seemed ...

Less than 24 hours later, he called me and was "in a jam" (which he wasn't really, he was lying while sitting at home watching a movie) and needed me to go and do something really physical and really time-consuming in a different county! In his mind, after giving me that gift and showing what a friend he really was, there was no way that I could turn him down.

In reality, he didn't want to do the physical labor or take the time to do it. Why should he? Especially, when in his mind, that "gift" would compel (read: "Guilt") me into doing it all for him! And, of course, he used the "You're doing me a real favor" angle as well. You see ... I had a pickup truck ... *That* was my "tool" for his use ... it ... and *me*.

See how they think and operate?

I won't go into all the details, but suffice it to say that I didn't fall into that trap either. I absolutely loved this amazing opportunity to actually study a real-life sociopath in action. Besides, he wasn't my first. But he was the first that I consciously studied.

A really scary fact about sociopaths is that they are everywhere!

Typically, they are so good at what they do, that those around them think they are totally   "normal" or "a really nice person". That is part of their persona ... a perfect eminence front.

For those of you who don't know ... nearly all serial killers are sociopaths. Some are psychopaths ... and the two are not far apart in diagnosis. The latter usually relishes more in the violence. The former, more in the ultimate feeling of power and control ... imposing their will on others, no matter the severity. Both usually appear completely normal, likable even, on the outside ... particularly the sociopath.

Both have no guilt or conscience whatsoever. The experience of what they do to their "victims" isn't personal towards their victim in their mind ... really ...

It is all about themselves.

The "victim", be it a murder victim, or someone being used as a "tool", is merely an "object" to be used by them as a means to their own end. They aren't seen as real "people" the way you or I would consider them. But this isn't a Psychiatry lesson, it is a study in them. It is about selfish folks … sociopaths or otherwise. Obviously, not all selfish folks are sociopaths and not all sociopaths are serial killers.

But … all sociopaths *are* selfish.

In their broken mind … the entire world revolves around them.

Everyone … and everything … is just that … *a thing* … an object for their use.

Even if not outwardly appearing so to those around them; if you watch long enough … or interact with them long enough … this trait will come shining through sooner or later.

And so it was with my friend.

In typical human response to his manipulations, I wanted revenge. Not literally, but it's in all of us to want to see someone that has used us or wronged us somehow, to be punished.

Trust me … Karma is a true bitch … even if you never see it, these folks do get theirs. So, don't sweat their hurtful abuses too hard. Brush it off, take the lesson and the realization of who/what they really are and move on.

Trust me, it's the easier path.

You *do not* want to get into a volley of "revenge" with a sociopath.

It's best to not play their game or let them in your life, or your head, and just slip off their radar. Let them go in peace and feel sorry for them. They will find another "victim" if you won't play along. Besides, they honestly can't help themselves. It is an illness … and, sadly, usually quite untreatable or curable.

Now, if you are a writer, like me, then you can give them their comeuppance on paper!

So to speak …

That is how this story came about … I was looking into all this portable recording tech gizmo-type stuff and I had this "friend" in my life trying to manipulate me into doing things for him.

In my odd-ball head, the two came together as this study of a true, selfish sociopath and his getting his payback ... but, with my twisted "Twilight-Zone"-influenced kind of bent. The protagonist isn't a representation of my friend, per se, He is a kind of an extreme conglomeration of all selfish-types and sociopaths.

The stop sign is a metaphoric symbol that he needs to stop this behavior ...

But he won't ... and ... it will catch up with him ... sooner or later.

The fact that he doesn't realize he is dead at first, is metaphoric for the fact that they just can't help themselves. In their world, everything is "normal" ... as long as they are getting their way.

Tell me true ...

Do you know one of these ... or have encountered one?

Now ... ask yourself... *Are you one*?

If you even pondered that you might be for *one* second ... then you aren't.

True sociopaths quite rarely, mostly never, recognize or acknowledge, their own condition. This makes it near incurable. It is truly one of the most fascinating and, sadly, untreatable conditions in human mental health.

They ... are born with this illness ... and we ... are all born with being selfish!

Isn't that odd?

Perpetrator

Gary French *hated* cigarettes … The smell of the break room turned his stomach. He could still see and *smell* the memory of his father smoking at the dinner table. Holding his breath and his nose, he poked his head in … looking for his partner. Officer Jay Skeen laughed at him while he snuffed out his cigar. Being well aware of Frenchy's distaste of tobacco, he teasingly blew his last pull across the table at him …

"Hey, smokestack … C'mon … We got a bad-guy walkin' around shootin' up the Franklin Street Mall!"

Jay's eyes went blank … He saw himself and his wife strolling down that very street … Just last weekend. He watched the trolley car whisk down the Cobblestone. He could see the birds hopping across the sidewalk to grab the bread his wife threw down for them as they luncheoned at the sidewalk café …

He *couldn't* see someone walking down the mall … *shooting* …

"Ya jokin' me?"

"Nope … just came in … He's walkin' down the street … shootin' everything."

Jay dropped the half-snuffed Hav-a-Tampa in the tuna can ashtray and grabbed his bottle of water.

He poured some over the cigar and stared at his partner. "*Everything*?" He asked.

Gary was nodding … "Everything … birds, storefronts, light posts …"

He turned his head and looked right at Jay. "*People* … EV-ER-Y thing!"

He wafted the strong smell of cigar back towards Jay as they turned out the doors toward the parking lot.

"Lucky us, huh …?" Frenchy quipped. " … *We* had to be three blocks away."

As they raced toward the heart of downtown Tampa, more information about the situation was streaming across the screen in their cruiser … Jay read it aloud while he toggled the siren switches … He let them go as his mouth dropped open on the last line he read.

"You just ain't *even* gonna believe this …"He announced, his Texan accent revealing his growing disbelief … His eyes couldn't leave the screen. " … There's a report that he's carrying a small boy …"

Frenchy's chin fell … He thought of his own two sons … trying to pry up one of the bricks in the cobblestone street, the last time he had taken them downtown for lunch.

His eyes turned from the road to his partner … "Now YER jokin' ME … right? … RIGHT?" His beckoning voice quivered, as Frenchy's own disbelief now exposed itself.

Jay shook his head and hoped that more info would come across the screen. Gary rolled his eyes as he turned his head back to the road … "Oh my God … What next …?" He sighed.

Jay's finger was tapping the refresh key … he still couldn't take his eyes from the screen.

"God I hope that's bad info"

"You can say that again Skeeny Baby …" Frenchy nodded. " … Any word on the perp?"

"Not yet"

"No ID … No nothin'?" Frenchy begged.

"Not yet."

"What about the hostage?"

"Nuh uh … nothin' at all." Jay's head shook, but his eyes stayed glued to the screen.

His finger never stopped tapping the refresh key as he toggled the siren at a car that wouldn't yield. He scowled through the windshield at the car …"Hey … Get his tag will ya?"

Jay made an evil face at the driver as they went around him. " … We'll see *you* later …YOU JERK!" Frenchy tried to grin as he looked, both ways, at the intersection of Tyler Avenue and Jefferson Street …

He could see his partner writing that guy a *stack* of tickets … But he just couldn't bring his lips to say it … He could not stop thinking about the poor boy … "How did this come to happen?"

The tires sang on the hot pavement as the cruiser tore around the corner and headed for Franklin Street …

Their siren echoed up and down the Cobblestone Street as the cruiser turned onto the mall … and stopped …

The two seasoned officers looked in amazement at the scene before them …

Gary looked at his watch …

"Twelve-forty." He muttered. He HAD to look again … Just to make sure it was indeed 12:40 … It was lunchtime … on Tuesday … in downtown Tampa … This Street *should* be packed …

But it wasn't today …

All they could see were bodies …

Scattered …

Everywhere …

Gary's foot eased off the brake pedal and let the cruiser idle forward …

Both men were scouring the street for the shooter. "My God … there must be twenty dead … maybe THIRTY!" Jay was nodding …" Neither could believe their eyes. Jay held the mic to his lips … "Ah, one-thirty-two, we've got at least two-dozen seventy-ones in the street, dispatch … maybe more … It looks like a war zone down here!"

Both the windshield *and* the driver's window shattered simultaneously as the first shot echoed down the empty mall … The sound of crashing glass drowned out the partners frightened cursing.

Gary hit the brake and slammed the shifter into reverse … " One-thirty-two … SHOTS FIRED!" The tires were smoking as the car rocketed backward up the street. "Repeat … We're being fired upon!"

"Copy, one-thirty-two … cover is code three"

Jay had drawn his weapon and was trying to peer out his open window to see where the shooter was …His blood ran cold when he saw them … There … in a doorway … not one block down … was the man … Holding a boy in his left arm … and waiving a pistol with the other.

The boy's arms were wrapped around the shooter's neck while his legs straddled him front and back. His pale, thin face was blank and expressionless … while the shooter's seemed wild-eyed and frightened.

"No way to get a shot off at the guy … He's holdin' that kid like a shield." Jay shouted.

"Well … he quit shootin' at us … maybe he just wants us to keep our distance." Frenchy reasoned.

He put the car in park at Tyler Ave. and switched the siren off. How he hated that sound … he found it to be the only curse of this job that he loved so much. He couldn't wait to make Detective and thereby use it a lot less … he hoped.

Frenchy's eyes grew wide as he stared at the shooter. "Oh my God Skeen … That's ol' Michael the perv!"

Jay replayed their last run-in with Michael in his mind as he squinted to confirm Gary's proclamation. They had listened to him trying to approach a small boy in the bathroom at a local park. His intentions were both clear and repulsive. Jay's teeth clenched together as he remembered the perv trying to run away as they identified themselves. Had they not been there trying to catch guys like Michael, "Lord only knows what would have happened to the poor boy." He thought.

As he remembered tackling Michael and placing him in cuffs, it occurred to him that Michael's rap sheet showed absolutely *no* penchant for violence … aside from running away, he gave no resistance …

"How on *Earth* … did he come to this?" He wondered.

Frenchy pushed open his door and drew his weapon in one motion … In one more motion, he was on one knee with his gun leveled at the shooter. He could feel the racing pulse in his arm as he rested it in the crook between the door and the car … The end of his barrel pinged against the chrome spotlight.

He looked through the car at Jay and told him to radio for the swat team … *And a sharpshooter …*

Jay radioed the scenario to dispatch and then clicked the knob over to public address mode.

"Michael, set your weapon down and let the boy go!" He commanded through the tinny-thin-sounding speaker tucked in the grill of the squad car.

The shooter lowered his revolver and looked at the boy … the boy looked at him and then the cruiser.

Turning his head back to them, Michael raised the pistol in slow motion …

He fired two rounds through the radiator and the steam blocked Frenchy's view for a moment. In between clouds of white steam, he saw the shooter tossing his gun across the cobblestone … His lungs exhaled in relief …"That's good punk, now put that poor boy down …" He thought. As the last of the steam billowed straight up, the partners couldn't believe their eyes … Michael had reached down to his waist and drew yet another pistol … this one was an automatic …

"Holy smokes Frenchy … You seein' what I'm seein'?"

"Oh yeah … I definitely concur, number one" It was his best Jean-Luc Picard impression.

Both were now staring at the array of handguns tucked into the waist of the shooter's pants.

"I count three … maybe four … *Besides* the one he's holdin' … I can't tell past the kid's legs!"

"Ditto!" … Frenchy's voice sounded monotone … He felt horrible for the helpless little boy.

Jay opened the Mic again … "If you just stop shooting … maybe … we can talk this out!"

The reply was four more shots through the flashing blue and red lights on top of the car … Pieces of the colored plastic went flying in every direction.

"Okay … Well … I guess THAT'S our answer!" Gary shouted.

He looked through the car at Jay and then scanned the broken glass that now covered the front seat. They could hear sirens coming from every direction … their wails echoed around them like a hurricane.

"Tell dispatch to keep them one block back for now … this jerk's libel to freak if he sees more units!"

Jay nodded and clicked back over to Comm from P.A. on the radio.

"One-thirty-two … this guy is highly unstable … and he *definitely* has a hostage!"

They looked at each other as he spoke … "A young male, approximately six to eight years old …" Jay took a deep breath as he tried to remember Michael's last name … but in the excitement, he couldn't.

"Perpetrator is a known Pedophile … First name Michael … approximately six foot tall, brown hair and eyes, late twenties to early thirties …" He paused and then un-keyed the Mic. He took another deep breath of the thick summer air. "Please advise covers to remain TWO blocks back."

They winked at each other as Jay finished … Two more shots ripped through Jay's door … He dove across the glass-covered seat. "Holy smokes, Dirty Harry!" He shouted, his voice showing fear for the first time today … "This friggin' guy's on a mission!" Neither of them heard the dispatcher's acknowledgment …

Gary couldn't take his eyes off of the boy … He kept looking at them … and then his captor. He felt the frustration in his chest and wished he could help him … he'd never felt so powerless before …

The boy's gaze was completely blank … He looked utterly terrified … yet he had a strange calmness.

"Poor kid is probably in shock" He thought.

Jay slid over the glass and back into position behind the door. Some of the glass showered over onto the aluminum door jam and down to the cobblestone at his feet. It crunched and crackled under his leather shoes. He readjusted his Kevlar vest and focused in on the unlikely pair that was now standing in the middle of the street. Gary wiped the sweat from his forehead and glanced back over at Jay.

"Y'all right?"

"I'll let ya know when this guy's DONE!" He snapped. "How ya think we should handle this?"

Frenchy turned his eyes back to the boy … "I guess we wait for the sharpshooter …" He shrugged.

" … We can't risk hitting the boy … Besides, it would seem he only fires if we try to talk to him … Let's just try and wait him out and see what happens …"

Jay was nodding in agreement before Gary finished his sentence. "Alright … but what if he starts shooting again?" He turned to look at Gary … "Or what if he shoots the hostage?" Gary never looked away from the boy … His voice was calm and professional …

"Then we take him down."

The shooter turned and began aimlessly shooting out the storefront to his right. The glass shattered and flooded the sidewalk with a resounding crash …

They could hear several women frantically screaming inside …

He stopped shooting for a moment and then turned his wrath on the traffic signal on the corner. They could hear errant rounds whizzing over their heads. Gary wiped the sweat from his palms … First one hand and then the other … on his blue uniform pants. He could see his wife ironing them as he dressed for duty this morning. He hoped he would see her this evening … *And,* that she *hadn't* come down *here* this afternoon to window shop … He never took his aim off of Michael.

Jay's eyes were caught by something moving in the foreground …

As were the shooters …

It was one of his victims … he was trying to crawl away. The trail of blood that he was leaving behind him told the partners he didn't have long …

"Stay still guy … Please … c'mon!" Jay pleaded. But the poor soul kept trying to crawl away.

When they looked back up to the shooter, he was in motion … He was staring at the poor crawler … And stomping towards him … When he was just a foot away, the shooter leveled the gun at his head …

Frenchy closed his eyes …"Oh, no … *don't* …"

The first shot drove the victim's head to the cobblestone … The next four made his body twitch in small spasms. Jay closed his eyes and shook his head … "How did this guy get so far OUT there!"? He was interrupted by two more loud pops.

" … I've *never* heard any reports of him being violent …" He shuddered at the last two rounds … "Sounds like a nine …" He reported. Frenchy agreed. "Yup, looks like a Glock Nineteen."

Jay rolled his eyes and shook his head in frustration … "Great … How many fired so far?"

"Eight or nine, I'm pretty sure."

They watched in horror as the shooter stepped over to an elderly woman who was lying just two yards from the crawler … She rolled over and screamed in hysteria … "NOOO … PLEASE DON'T SHOOT ME!" She pleaded.

She had been playing dead, but panicked when he got so close … Michael raised his pistol and fired six rounds into her head … She wasn't moving after the first two. The partners looked on in horror as he threw the empty gun at her bloody face and drew another weapon … a blue steel revolver.

He spun around in the street and randomly emptied it into the bodies that were strewn around him … as if he were trying to make sure they were all dead. The partners shook their heads in disgust …

The boy's lower lip stuck out … as though he were going to cry.

After the sixth round, Michael slammed the pistol onto the crawler's head with a dull thud. Jay winced at the splashing blood. Fifteen years on the streets hadn't hardened him enough for the scene that was unfolding before him. The shooter reached to the back of his waist and drew another automatic.

Gary beaded the shooter's head into his sights … His chest felt warm and tight … like it was turning to stone … He had a shot … But … what if the shooter turned or changed direction?

He just *couldn't* risk hitting the poor little boy … Besides … At the moment, it would seem, only Skeen and he was in immediate danger … Unless that is … someone *else* was playing dead. His sweaty finger eased off of the trigger …

"Where's the damn sharpshooter?" He snapped. Jay shook his head and reached for the microphone.

He watched the shooter walk back to the intersection of Franklin and Cass Street as he pleaded with the dispatcher for the whereabouts of the sharpshooter.

"One-thirty-two … two-fifty-six is en route." Came the dispatcher's reply …

Frenchy's voice was beginning to show his tension … "Tell 'em ta hurry will ya?"

Jay relayed the last few moments of their ordeal to dispatch … in vulgar, graphic detail … at this moment, he could care less about radio etiquette … He *needed* dispatch to understand the urgency of their requests.

He pleaded for them to rush the Sharpshooter to the scene. "One-thirty-two … two-fifty-six is en route." The dispatcher repeated.

Both men rolled their eyes in frustration as Jay tossed the Mic, in disgust, onto the glass-covered front seat. "Well at least he used the hand-cannon on the seventy-ones"

"I know … that sounded like a three-fifty-seven …" Jay reckoned.

"At least!" Frenchy agreed. He stuck out his lower lip and blew a sigh across his face … it was a *very* balmy Florida afternoon.

The shooter looked up and around at the skyscrapers behind him. He and the boy looked at each other and then he turned and began firing at the buildings … To Gary, he looked like a tiny helpless being, trying to thwart huge, looming assailants. They all watched the glass fall … in silence … to the sidewalks in the distance. Jay envisioned the painting of David and Goliath in his son's bible.

"I can't see the weapon, but I think that's eight shots!" Frenchy yelled over the ringing booms of the gun.

"Eight it is …" Jay yelled back. " … It sounds like a three-eighty … Maybe another nine!" Gary nodded. The shooter fired two more rounds and then threw the gun, over-arm, at the closest tower … He looked like David; slinging the stone at Goliath … It fell hopelessly short …

Before he turned around, he had already drawn another weapon … A large chrome automatic … This one had a long barrel … And a laser sight. Both partners took a deep gulp of humid summer air …

"Oh, greeeat … " Frenchy lamented. " … I sure hope that's a twenty-two target pistol!"

Jay's eyes were wide with anticipation … "Me too buddy!"

Their hopes were quickly dashed as the captor opened fire on the trolley car that had crashed into a park bench and came to rest. He was shooting at the head of the already dead driver. Michael looked at the boy and then began shooting out the windows of the trolley. Bodies that were slumped against the windows were falling away into the aisle of the bus. The partners could feel the concussion of the high-powered weapon …

"Definitely a forty-four auto-mag!" Frenchy shouted over the din of the hand cannon.

"Eight shots fired of a possible … Make that *likely* … twelve … " Jay concurred.

"Let's hope he doesn't turn that laser on us!"

The shooter stopped firing and turned his glare towards the cruiser …

Frenchy swore he could see the fear in his eyes as he raised his now shaking hand in their direction …

Without speaking, the partners dove, in unison, toward the back of the cruiser as they listened to the next four shots tear into it … The impact of the huge rounds jolted the car like bb's hitting an aluminum can.

"Now … That one's empty … ya okay?" Jay was panting with a little panic. His partner was looking towards the sky … "Fine … THAT was TOO close …"

Gary laid out on the cobblestone and peered under the car for the position of the shooter. He was walking away slowly in the center of the street. He snapped up and leveled his weapon at the back of his head …

"Don't try it, my brother … think of the kid." Jay begged, but it was too late … Frenchy was already telling himself not to do it. He let out a frustrated sigh and lowered his weapon.

The shooter turned around and lobbed the now empty pistol at the cruiser … both men ducked.

It skipped off the hood and crashed into the already broken windshield. They peered around the car and saw the shooter draw what seemed to be his last weapon from his waist.

"I think he's almost out of firepower buddy … Maybe we can reason with him now …" Again, without talking, they crept back up to their positions behind the doors of the cruiser.

"I can't see any more weapons." Jay reported.

"Me neither … Wait'll he turns around again." Frenchy snapped in an urgent whisper.

They watched the boy turn back and look at them, as the shooter carried him back to the intersection.

When he reached the manhole cover in the center of it, he stopped and looked at the boy …

Frenchy's heart raced … "Oh … NO … God … PLEASE!" He begged.

The shooter turned slowly around and glared at them again.

He looked more desperate than before … like he *knew* these moments were coming to an end …

Jay grabbed the mic again … switched the radio back to public address and began shouting …

"C'mon Michael … you can't keep shooting forever … Just put the gun down and let the boy go … We'll get you all the help we can … NO ONE wants to hurt you … I promise, I swear."

The shooter was sweating profusely as he looked up into the searing Tampa sun. He wiped his brow and closed his eyes to the light breeze that caressed his face. His long, curly hair wafted behind him … He opened his eyes and looked at the boy.

The boy looked back at the officers … Frenchy called out to the child as loud as he could …

"You alright son?"

The boy looked back into Frenchy's eyes …

Frenchy was trying to make the perv see the small prisoner as a person and not an object … He was trying to make the boy talk …

His expression was still completely blank … "Poor thing, he *must* be in shock from all this." He thought.

Gary's eyes filled with terror as he watched the shooter slowly raise the gun up to the small boy's chest …

Neither partner could exhale …

The boy turned to the shooter and grabbed the barrel, pushing it away, back towards *his* chest … The shot sounded muffled as the shooter collapsed backward to the ground in a heap.

Both men bolted around the cruiser doors, keeping their weapons trained on the shooter …

The boy was standing over him with his hands on his waist … staring.

"You get the perp … I got the boy!" Jay shouted as they quick-stepped over to them.

"You got it!" Frenchy snapped, as he stepped between the shooter and the gun.

He kicked it away behind him and watched Jay snatch the boy up and carry him towards the battered, still smoking, police cruiser … Letting out a long sigh of relief, he looked down at Michael … Gary holstered his weapon and knelt down on one knee next to him … squinting into his glazed eyes …

He patted him down as best he could for more weapons or maybe some identification …

Nothing …

Nothing that was going to help make some sort of sense out of *any* of this day …

Then their eyes met again …

The shooter was shaking …

Gary spoke through gritted teeth …

"What were you doin' Michael … And WHAT … *exactly* … IS your problem?" He yelled.

The shooter raised his head off the Cobblestone Street …

Grabbing up at Gary's uniform, he was trying to take a deep, gurgling breath …

He looked straight up into Frenchy's eyes …

His gaze froze Frenchy solid …

He was coughing up blood as he spoke …

"Leave … the boy … ALONE!" was all he said, as his head fell back on the bricks with a thud.

The sound of Michael's death rattle was interrupted by the sound of Jay's service weapon …

Gary pivoted on his toes in terror …

Jay was coming back down the street … straight towards him …

Still holding the boy …

He was taking potshots at a few of the bodies that were strewn across the mall.

Then … he stopped … a few feet away … He now had the same frightened stare that Michael had had only moments before …

Officer Jay Skeen spun around to Frenchy and raised the six-shot revolver up to his partner's forehead …

Officer Gary French recounted the last five shots in his mind … all Jay's … He could *feel* the warm barrel between his eyes …

He looked up at the boy's still stony face …

The boy looked back down at him …

And smiled.

Okay, dear Reader, I can *hear* your wheels turning now …

I can *see* you shaking your head at this page …

"Where … among all that horror and violence … could there *possibly* be a message … of *any* kind, about us and who we are? You've just crossed the line Mr. Gaines. There may be violent, bad peoples out there … but they do *not* represent mankind as a whole!"

Oooh, dear Reader … you are so … *so* … very wrong. The child in that story is a very telling representation of something inside all of us … *especially* when we are children. On top of that … I have my own reasoning or philosophy about it. Of course … I'm going to explain *that* as we go here.

Anyone who has been bullied as a child … or even witnessed children bullying, first hand, can bear witness to this thing that I'm talking about. It happens every day, all over the world. Children, without exception, can be some of the most vicious, cruel humans ever. Part of our schooling and being raised by parents is, normally, to *not* be a bully … to be nice to others … The Golden Rule and so-forth. There isn't a culture or religion on Earth that does *not* teach this.

For lack of a better way to put it … it is part of our "training" to become nice, healthy, well-adjusted adults. Remember that word … *Training* … because I am going somewhere with this. We will be there soon enough. But first, I want to really expound on this "cruelty-of-children" thing.

When I was a child, I was bullied. I was a skinny, short, slight, awkward child … until I reached puberty. But prior to that, I was beaten, terrorized and tormented to the point where I had to have two sets of school books … one at school and one for doing homework that was kept on our dining room table.

The school came up with this solution … as my poor mother couldn't afford to keep *buying* schoolbooks because my tormentors kept throwing them out of the school bus window. In those days, little was done about this. They wrote it off as "kids being kids" and would just give a verbal chastising, at best.

Then there was the scheduled Monday drive to school. God, I loved that day. It was the one of ten trips to and from school per week, where I didn't have to be tormented. She had to drive me because she had to bring my weekly school lunch money in and drop it off in the office.

She had 5 days lunch money, each day in a separate envelope with the day of the week, the amount and my name on it. These were all put inside a larger, brown mailer envelope, again, with my name and the words "Lunch Money" on it.

Just *seeing* those words every day when I collected my lunch money from the lady in the office were an embarrassment to me. I *hated* reading those words. They reminded me of the torment ... the torment that they put me through ... *and* the torment my Mother suffered along with me.

I *used* to bring my lunch, but after countless glass thermos liners being smashed because they would take my lunch box and hit me with it, sending my milk all through the lunch box ... not only breaking the thermos, but soiling my lunch as well ... I now ate school lunch every day. My Mom had deduced it was actually cheaper than replacing all the thermoses and lunch boxes.

Before that, many, many days, I had no lunch at school, maybe just a piece of fruit. The inside of my lunch box would be a smelly, mushy mess that was sometimes so putrid from milk-soaked sandwiches, spoiled from the Florida heat, that the same tormentors would throw that out the school bus windows with my books because it was smelling up the bus.

There are more stories of what happened to me ... but you get the picture.

Humans ... especially children, can make suffering and misery like no other animal ... and even take great joy in doing so. It seems inexplicable ... and yet, it happens day after day ... everywhere.

Nowadays, with the Internet and (Anti)social media, we have bullying at epic proportions that leads kids to do *unspeakable* things ... Things that we never dreamed of happening just a few short decades ago ... but, we will touch on that in another write.

One day, my best friend's wife, Sallie, had given me a copy of "Conversations With God: An Uncommon Dialog", by Neale Donald Walsh. I have to admit, I wasn't hiding my smirk very well when she handed it to me. She grinned a bit with me and told me she *knew* I would not only like it, but that I would *get it* as well. Trusting her implicitly, I sat down on my couch and started reading as soon as she left. I didn't put it down until I'd read it all the way through. It isn't a long read, just over 200 pages.

I was a bit taken aback. Here is this man, writing that he asked God questions and that he *answered* him. I'll not go into it all, but I will implore you to read it. Take from it what you will. What is said in the book ... by "God" ... is nothing less than fascinating.

Let me clarify something here ... This isn't a bible-thumping, fire and brimstone, "God is great" religious book. It has some *very interesting* questions and some even more interesting answers.

Kudos to the Author ...

I mean ... if allowed to ask questions of God ... what would *you* ask? Now, some of his questions were the predictable ones ... "Why are we here?" and the like. But some were much more clever.

However ... It was the *answers* that took me.

Especially the answer to "Why are we here?"

I mean ... who *hasn't* pondered *that* question?

The response is that we are *all* deities.

Gods ... all of us.

And ... that we are put here to learn how to be just that ... Gods.

The "God" in this book, explains that we need to come here first, because even God's are born with "original sin". That is to say that in our youth, we don't understand the true difference between right and wrong. We don't grasp the concepts of "Forever" or "Death" or even "Guilt" ... at first.

It is here ... this world ... this realm ... where we learn Humility, Love, Sorrow, Pain, Joy and all the other concepts that need to be completely understood *before* we can be bestowed with the omnipotent abilities of a "God".

It is here ... in essence ... that we are being "*Trained* to be Gods".

It makes an odd sort of sense, if you accept it. After all ... how could you give these abilities recklessly to a child deity, that could, if provoked, clap his hands and make all existence *vanish*? He is too young to understand the concept … *or* the ramifications of "forever". So, as young deities, we are sent here over and over until what we perceive as the soul, "learns" to be a good, well-heeled "God".

A God that understand benevolence and won't abuse his ability … destroying all of existence in a childish tantrum or destroying races and worlds … because he doesn't deem them worthy.

Such a deep and interesting concept, huh Reader?

I thought so too.

Imagine that …

We are *all* … Gods!

Do I actually believe this?

I can't say … Firstly, I would never make such conjecture. I was raised a Southern Baptist and have been exposed to many religions and theories …

But, given the concept, it is not one that I wouldn't consider. I am pretty open minded. Secondly, I am also very analytical. I need to be shown things to believe them. But when you look around at the world, and you truly ponder that concept, it can actually have a ring of truth come from it.

If you can get your head around us being "Gods", then it can actually makes sense, when explaining "why we are here". There are many other concepts in that series of 3 books. But the first book really touched me. Especially the "Why are we here?" question and its answer.

I was thinking about how, when I was a kid, I loved playing Army and Cowboys. That's what boys my age did in those days. We didn't have video games, cable TV or computers … we had chemistry sets … and GI Joe's … Matchbox or Hot Wheel cars … and, more often than not, toy guns.

After you finish gasping, remember … this was a much gentler time … a much simpler time. We, as Humans, have lost so much of our innocence since that time, that I often fear for us as a species.

Anyway ... we used to "shoot" each other on a daily basis. Either as a cowboy or as a soldier. Now this sounds innocent enough, as we were *pretending* ...

Still ... we were *killing* each other with great joy. The thought of our pals not getting up to run home for supper never entered our minds. We never considered the ramifications or the guilt of our actions like a *real* soldier would. We were too young to have those emotions influence us and our actions.

I got to thinking about that after reading that book and this short story came to me, in its entirety. I wanted to have the Cops ... and therefore ... the reader ... see the poor child as the victim, *not* the "Perpetrator" because ... well ... he *must* be ... right? Children don't walk down streets, *shooting* people.

Well, if freely given that option, *or* ... the ability to make another person do that, they may very well do just that.

Why not?

It might be fun!

That's the way a child thinks. It is also a demonstration in the way children don't fear the repercussions of their actions. I wanted the Cops ... *and* the reader, to realize this ... only when it was way too late.

It is my way of demonstrating this concept about how, if a child is given the ability to "make" someone kill randomly, they may well do just that ... and they might even be *amused* by it. In its own way, there is such a truth to "God's" answer to that age-old question in that book.

If it were true, then *surely* ... we would all indeed need the training we receive here first ... *before* we are given this omnipotent power.

Is it reality?

Are we really deities, here living these lives to learn how to behave as a "proper" God?

Who knows?

But it made for a fun ... if not *creepy* ... short story!

The Way I See It

On Clouds ...

"Since I was pretty young ... I've had a strange fascination with clouds.
Now that I'm older, I often ponder how much our very lives
are so much like them.
It is sad that when most folks mention them,
it is in the context of " ... a dark cloud over my head" or some such idiom ...
and so very telling that as we age, we notice them less and less.

True ... dark clouds bring rain ...
But why is this always seen as a negative connotation?
Without rain, nothing can grow or even survive.

When I think of clouds, I like to think of all that they bring us ...
They can even stir our very imagination on a lazy day in a park.
Children see clowns and puppies in them.
Couples in moments of romance see hearts and flowers and such ...
while elderly people might see the faces of friends and family
that they love or miss.

Every morning and every evening, we revel in amazement
as they become the palettes for breathtaking moments painted by the Sun.
We also sigh in relief under these puffy umbrellas of white
when they hide us from its heat in the day.
They do so many things for us ... They bring us so many beauties
and reliefs and even things that are essential to our very existence.

And yet ... typically ... we take them for granted ...
When we do refer to them, or think of them ...
it is negatively somehow, more often than not ...
We rarely notice them ... as they silently drift past us ...
just like everything and everyone around us."

~Jeff Gaines

Why Me?

"Sometimes ... I lie awake at night and ask "Why me?" Then a voice usually answers "Nothing personal, your name just happened to come up"."

~Charles M. Schultz

Jamaica, Jamaica!

"One Love ... One heart ... Let's get together and feel alright."
-Robert Nesta Marley

Take a deep breath ...

No, seriously ...

No breath you *ever* take will be like the one that you take when you look out over her azure and aquamarine blue waters or her lush green hills ...

Now, let it out.

No breath you *ever* let out will be like the one that you let out when you listen to one of her waterfalls or finally meet and make friends with just one of her incredible people.

Unless you go there ...

Your lungs will *never* be filled with the air from that blessed place like mine have been.

It's sweeter ...

Thicker ...

Spicier ...

The place I'm speaking of isn't Heaven ... and it isn't Utopia ... or even the Garden of Eden.

If you live anywhere in the United States ... It's only a plane ride or two away. And if you're really lucky, then you live in the southeastern U.S. and you can get there on a leisurely cruise ship.

Hear me now ... Once you've been there, it stays with you ... *inside* you ... *forever.*

You never *really* leave it ... It never *really* leaves you. So even when you are away from her, all you have to do is close your eyes ... and breathe.

I'm talking about ... ***Jamaica!***

It's my favorite place in the whole world ... Bar None.

I love living in west central Florida. The Tampa Bay area, without a doubt, is one of the coolest places to live in the country ... in the world possibly.

I haven't been everywhere, so I'm not qualified to decide thee coolest place to live in the world. I have however, been to every state in the continental U.S. as well as all the Canadian Provinces and most of Europe. On top of that, I've been to the Bahamas, Saint Lucia, Aruba, Puerto Rico, Barbados, Turks and Caicos, Trinidad and well … you get the picture. I have found wondrous beauty and fascinating people everywhere I've went.

Each island and country … each state even … having it's own unique people and characteristics that made them a joy to discover and explore. I've left a piece of myself in each of these destinations and they, in turn, have left a mark on me as well. All of these places and the people who inhabit them are in me forever. I can only hope that I've left such a mark in the spots I've visited and maybe in some of the souls that I've had the joy of meeting along the way.

Only a few places in my travels have left me with a bad taste in my mouth. I'll not name them here. I hate to throw stones. Besides … This piece is about *JOY!*

Remember that word … *JOY*

When you finally arrive in Jamaica, and I don't mean the "Touristy-everything-you-see-in-the-travel-ads" Jamaica. I mean the "Leave-the-hotel-on-foot-and-walk-down-the-road-for-some-fresh-cut-sugarcane-and-cold-coconut-milk-at-the-roadside-vendor" Jamaica … You will discover a joy that you've only dreamed of all your life.

But that's not all … While you stand on the edge of that road … Be it in Trelawny or Sav-La-Mar, Negril or Port Antonio and you listen to the tropical breeze in the trees over your head, chewing on your 'cane, sipping your coconut milk … Something wonderful will happen …

It will discover *you.*

Like the sun that gleams in the eyes of her people …

Like the soft, warm sand between your toes …

Like her hypnotic rhythms that echo through the air … Night and Day.

You see here … you make friends with these things … You have no choice. The people here learned it a century ago …

You're here … *enjoy* it.

There's nowhere you *have* to be … *right now.*

Nothing *needs* to be done … *right now.*

I think whomever coined the phrase "*Wherever you go, there you are.*" Did so in Jamaica.

I'm rather fond of telling people that " ... You can have fun with me in a cardboard box." What I mean by that is that I know who I am. I have found myself and am very comfortable with what I've discovered. I can find fun most anywhere I am.

Of course, I aspire to have and do more ... *But* ... I'm not going to die while I wait.

John Donne once said, "No man is an island."

I disagree, in a manner of speaking ...

I agree that as a species, we *are* all one ...

But ... we are, in our own way, as individuals, *each* an island unto ourselves ...

Our world an ocean ...

Who we are is defined by the size and shape of our "island". Some are large, with the ability to take on and handle many tasks and tests. While others are sleek and beautiful to behold so many "do" for them in return for being allowed to relish in their beauty. And still others are imposing and brutal, hiding a fear of what the others have ... know ... or are capable of doing. This ocean gives us the space we need to learn and grow, but some would like to consume it all up in a most awful game of "I, Me, Mine".

There is much to learn here on this magical isle ...

About life ...

About pain ...

About truth ...

About politics ...

About sorrow ...

About history ...

About strength ...

About passion ...

About injustice ...

About love ...

About perseverance ...

About the rest of the world ...

But, more importantly than any of these things ...

If you don't just come here to be a tourist … You will learn about yourself.

You will discover each other … *You* and this beautiful Island.

Not that being a tourist is a bad thing … Jamaica's number one source of income is tourism. It's just that when you do only *"touristy"* things, you are probably not alone. Nor are you likely to discover someone who could become a lifelong friend. Here, being a tourist is to learn about Jamaica, *not* being one is to learn about your self …

The people around your tour, more than likely, will be doing a job or being a tourist, just like you. There's nothing spiritual about riding around on a bus with a bunch of people taking pictures and asking a lot of questions. One of the best ways to "discover" who you are, is to be alone … not *lonely* … Alone.

Listen to your inner voice … and breathe.

Sometimes couples, close friends or even families come undone because they fail to give each other the space each needs to grow. Eventually, their "inner self" regresses enough to lash out and make this space. Without understanding why, they have inadvertently driven themselves apart, all in the name of trying to be "who they are". When I read history books, I theorize that this anomaly has destroyed *races* and *nations* …

Sometimes, we *need* to be alone. Like wolves or dolphins, we are, in essence, pack animals. We instinctively hate to be alone and will go to great lengths to be in another human's company. Like some folk's go to sleep with the radio or T.V. on, just the sound of another human voice can be comfort enough to send us blissfully into slumber. The irony here is that we will also go to great lengths to be alone. Sometimes the drone of cars, machines and yes, even other people, can overwhelm us … clouding or even drowning out our all important inner voice.

That voice being the entity that is who we are. It is all seeing … All understanding … All hearing … All loving. We may not always hear or understand it, but it is what and who we are … What we will always be … Some might call it the inner child.

And like all other living beings … it gains knowledge and, more importantly, experiences … So, like a child, it must grow.

The knowledge …

The memories … and the wisdom of life that they bring us, is tangible. These things have substance and mass. We may repress them … forget them even. But … they *never* go away. As they amass in our souls, they expand. That is how we grow. If you are looking for that child, I think you can find it in Jamaica.

If you still know that child and would like a growth spurt or even a place to start that growth anew ...

Come to Jamaica ...

I promise you, if you let go of all you think and do at home, fall into the pace of "Island time" and, most importantly ... *Let her in* ... Jamaica will change you forever.

When you come home from the trip where this happens to you, you will know. The only way I can describe it is to say that when you try to reintegrate into the world you've always known, it will be a bit of a task. Believe it or not, you will actually feel like you're still there ... In Jamaica.

Breathe ...

From the other side of the fence, the experience is the same. When you first arrive on her shores, you are still back where you came from, so to speak. Don't be ashamed. You don't know the difference ... *yet*.

In your world, you've been conditioned to be who and what it takes to survive. You have your accent and your slang terms, your favorite foods and your favorite music and pub.

All these "learned behaviors" along with your odd idiosyncrasies and cute little habits make you "*You*".

This is exactly where I've been going here ... You are only "*You*" when in "your" element.

"You can take the boy out the neighborhood, but you can't take the neighborhood out of the boy" so to speak. But, just being "*You*" when you are at home ... in your element, doesn't mean that you've discovered "*You*". In fact, I think that being molded by a certain place or group of people, a "pack" if you will, pushes you away from being or knowing the real you and into a mold built by your surroundings.

Tell me true ...

How many times have you snuck away to the rooftop ...

Or driven alone in the country with the radio off ...

Or just wandered off for a walk ... or a long shower ... alone? That is your inner-self doing it's thing ... Growing.

Breathe ...

The solace you feel in those moments is your inner-self expanding. Relish in it. It is one of the healthiest things you can do for yourself. That's where "Island Time" comes in. While you are used to making a call or driving up the block to get what you need "right now"; it doesn't quite happen that way here. Even in their best resorts. The pace here is slower ... *MUCH* slower.

It should be ... it *has* to be. It's not just a pace ... or a frame of mind ... It's a way of life. You aren't at home any more. Nothing happens with the snap of your fingers ... it happens in three or four snaps ... okay , Maybe five or six.

Keep snapping ... when it falls into the beat of the song in the background *unnoticed* ... you're almost there.

The people here learned long ago that slow perseverance will get you through anything ... and they have been through so much ... You will just never know ... until you go there. Go there. And while you're waiting a little longer on your cocktail or your food, look around ... think ... and breathe.

Think about how far away you are from what drove you to come here in the first place. Think about how far away you are from work, the kids, the farm, the traffic, the weather, the cell phone, the traffic ... and above all ...

Breathe ...

Oh, there's your cocktail now ... See? That wasn't so bad ... Was it?

As you linger here, you will get used to it. You will understand that the Jamaicans aren't rude or lazy as some of your ignorant, less open-minded friends who came here before you have warned that you they are. It isn't so. These people who speak badly of all Jamaicans couldn't grasp the concept of "Island time" because they were still "at home". I'll bet anything you can name that they never discovered themselves or Jamaica on their trip. Not just a waste of money ... An even bigger waste of time.

No disrespect to Walter Elias, but they may as well have went to Disney World ...

Entertainment ... at it's best.

Self-discovery ... *not* on your best day.

Here we have yet another irony. If someone you know speaks badly of the Jamaicans, or calls them rude or lazy, I'll bet more of anything you can name that *they* were the ones who were crass or "Holier than thou" with the Jamaicans *first* ... Whining about how long it took to get something or how long it took for the waitress to take their order or bring their coffee refill. What they failed to learn is that *that* isn't the way things work here ...

"Island Time" prevails.

"Soon come, Mon" … And soon it *will* come … Mon.

But while you wait … Breathe.

What's your hurry anyway?

The beach isn't going anywhere … nor is the waterfall up the road or the open-air market downtown. Now maybe the Reggae festival *does* start at sunset or maybe it's even *that* very sunset that you're trying to off rush to … but remember, "When in Rome, do as the Romans do." So it's *your* fault, *not* the Jamaican waitresses fault, that you are now waiting in "Island Time" for your drink or your food. Still *more* irony: More often than not, these people speak rudely to the Jamaicans first and then run home to tell it the *other* way around.

Breathe …

Don't rush anything here … it defeats the purpose.

Trust me, I've been here more than forty times. I've been almost everywhere on the island. I drive when I come here. *That* is another story for another time. I've sat in the hills of cockpit country; I've eaten cherries, yes *cherries*, in a man's yard in the high country near Savannah-Del-Mar with my friend John Swaby. The Jamaicans call it "Sav-la-mar". I've driven the high road over the Blue Mountains from "Town" (Kingston) all the way to "Mobay" (Montego Bay). It was absolutely breathtaking.

The first time I went to Jamaica, I went by myself. I've always been the adventurer. But I had no idea what I was in for. I stayed two days in Mobay at the Wexford Hotel on Gloucester Ave, and then I went out to Negril for four more days at Hedonism II. In Mobay, I wandered over to Walter's Bar and Grill for a Red Stripe or a Dragon Stout and maybe a bowl of Pumpkin soup. During those two nights partying in the hot spots down by the water, I kept finding myself back at Walter's trying to escape the loud goings-on.

I had heard so much about Negril (and its even *slower* pace) that I woke up on the third morning, packed up my stuff and went down to the street to get a cab. Two hours and seventy-five bucks later, I was at Hedonism. I was so drunk by the time I got there that the desk clerk took my bags and told me to go hit the buffet so I could " … wake up a likkle". Well, I used to be somewhat of a professional drinker and I walked right past the food to the world famous "all-you-can-drink" bar and proceeded to drink some more …

When I woke up (read: came to) the next morning, I was in a hammock down by the beach of the hotel. There was a security guard asking me if I was all right. He'd noticed that I wasn't wearing my room key around my neck or my wrist and he wondered if I was the "missing" gentleman from the night before (I didn't have one, as I'd not checked in yet!).

I silently hoped I wasn't in trouble … and I confessed to him that I was indeed the "missing" guy.

The eight beer glasses (five empty, three full) in the sand around my hammock told him the rest of the story. He didn't ask for an explanation. I tried to gather up the glasses to clean up my mess and he told me that I didn't have to worry " … bout dem tings here." He just smiled and showed me the way to the front desk.

The Jamaicans are not rude. They are some of the most friendly, inviting people in the world. Now get this, not only was all my cash still intact in my pocket and my luggage safe behind the front desk … they wouldn't *let* me pay for my stay in the hammock or the free beer … They said they loved taking care of me and that was that.

He checked me into a room and the rest of my adventure began. (I *wish* I could remember what happened after I got there! The whole time I was at Hedonism, the staff smiled and whispered when they saw me coming.) Try any of *that* at the Times Square Marriott or the Los Angeles Four Season's!

In those next few days, I met a Rastafarian cabby outside the gate of the hotel; his name was Rasta Errol. He was *so* cool; he took me to Rick's Café and he almost died when he watched me jump from the cliffs there. (He didn't think I would do it.) I could see the whites of his widened eyes forty feet below me as he watched me jump.

Later, he took me to little food shops and roadside stands. The next day, he took me up into the hills of cockpit country to see … Well, "Tings" … (Read: *illegal* "Tings").

But the best part of it all was that he let me just "Hang". I'd sit at the cabstand with him and try to understand the banter of Patois between him and some of the other locals as they played Dominoes. They'd constantly reassure me that they weren't talking about me and I'd reassure *them* I wasn't paranoid. (This *filled* them with laughter. You see? Jamaican people are *not* rude!)

We ran errands for his wife, fixed his car, he even took me around to meet some of his family … All for no charge. He could see that I wasn't trying to be a tourist. He truly appreciated my being "real", but more importantly, he respected it. I even rode along with some of his fares. I didn't care; the guy needed to feed six kids!

I guess growing up in a tourist mecca like Florida; you get used to *not* being a tourist. Life in Florida is pretty laid back, so just hanging around in Jamaica seemed pretty natural to me. I wanted to eat her food, know her people, her customs, her language and her culture … I wanted to know her.

While I was there I did just that, I found all those things … and *they* found me … I also found myself … I was comfortable to just "be" there … And, I learned … anywhere else for that matter.

Everyting Criss' …

Everyting Irie …

No problem Mon …

She had found *me* …

When I came back from that trip I was different. My friends said so. My family said so. My girlfriend said so. I had a little trouble keeping up with things because, like I said before, I was still there … in Jamaica.

It wasn't until seven years later that I could go back. I would hear the commercials or listen to some reggae and long to be back there, but fate had dealt me some blows … I had neither the time nor the wherewithal to go back. It was bearable though … all I had to do was close my eyes and … breathe.

If the Island, for some reason, doesn't sink into your soul like it has mine, then I promise you her people surely will. The Jamaican motto is "Out of many, One people." I think this should be the motto for the whole planet. But, leave it to the Jamaicans to come up with it first. This tiny island, one-hundred and twenty-two miles long, fifty-two miles wide has changed and educated many people and things on this huge planet … Think not? Try some of these things out and *then* tell me what you think …

Reggae Music … A style recognized and adored the world over.

Jamaica Blue Mountain Coffee … Arguably the finest, *definitely* one of the rarest and most expensive coffee's in the world.

James Bond … Ian Fleming drew this invincible spy's name from a Jamaican book and penned all these stories at his home in Jamaica!

Getting the idea?

Good, because I could fill this page with people and things that are everyday words in the rest of the world that have somehow emanated out of this tiny little island nation in one way or another …

What an energy!

The first time I wandered into the square in downtown Mobay, I will never forget the first thing I noticed. Now, I don't have to tell you that times are tough here. More people here are "have-not's" than there are "do-have's". But when you go there, sit down while you're waiting for a drink and watch the "pickney's" (children). They play and laugh on every street. You'll see them on the side of the road and at the seaside.

A lot of them have never owned a pair of shoes or a matching outfit in their whole lives. Most of them have never owned a bicycle, or woke up on Christmas morning to a tree with tons of presents under it. It's not that they miss these things *per se'* ... it's that they are children ... And like the inner child inside of you, it doesn't really matter to them. Coveting things is a *learned behavior.*

From their youth they learn to discover themselves ... without the trappings of western "civilization".

This is something that the Jamaicans and a lot of other less "blessed" nations have up on all of us supposedly "more prosperous" nations ... We merely *assume* that they are ignorant ... they *know* that we are! Most of us are *so* arrogant that we miss this entirely ... Thinking that because they are not as "well off" as we are, that somehow they are inferior and we are superior.

HA!

I'll tell you what ... In a battle scenario where all combatants were unarmed and had to survive the fight through wit, ingenuity, perseverance and intuition, I'd take an army of Jamaicans over the best trained soldiers in the world ... Any time ... *every time.*

And we would *win* that battle.

The thing that struck me so hard in the square that day was the pickney's smiles. No matter where you see them, no matter what you see them up to, you will almost always see them doing one thing ... Smiling.

They are content.

I'm sure they aspire to do and have more like everyone else ... *But* as I said before ... they know they are not going to die while they wait.

That is the biggest lesson that Jamaica has to share with many of us. It is a badly needed lesson, indeed. We take so much for granted. We take each other for granted. Come to Jamaica and see what it's like to have a "tough life" and then go home and see if it doesn't make you appreciate all the comforts that we so readily have right here at our disposal ...

Like shoes ...

Running water ...

Telephones, TVs, dishwasher's, microwaves …

Air conditioning …

Not that there aren't many who do have some, most or all of these things here in Jamaica *but* … There are far too many who do not …

Tell you what …

How 'bout you let me and my buds come by your house and take all these things away from you for a week … Okay? Then, let us drop back by and rudely whine and complain when you don't bring our cocktail or our second cup of coffee when *we* thought you should bring it!

Would you feel a little rude … or dare I say it … *angry?*

An old Native American saying dictates: "Do not judge a brave until you have walked for a day in his moccasins." I have never walked in the shoes of a Jamaican.

But I have met, worked and hung around with enough of them to know that I love and respect them with all my heart. They don't need your pity either. Trust me, they don't want it. They are as proud a people as any. And *remember* … they don't miss the things we covet most days of our pampered lives.

But, they are also very misunderstood by so many people. People who probably will never make friends with their own inner child …

Or understand "Island Time" …

Or Joy …

Or for that matter … *Themselves.*

Now close your eyes … and breathe.

Come … and find Joy …

Come … and find that inner child …

Come … and find yourself …

Come to Jamaica …

Let *her* discover *you.*

~**Jeff Gaines**
October 14th & 15th 2002
Port Richey, Florida.
(Wishing he was up on Richmond Hill!)

"To awaken quite alone in a strange town is one of the most pleasant sensations in the world."
~ Freya Stark

As you can tell, I really Love Jamaica. It is unlike anywhere else I have ever been. I know that this was written many moons ago and things change. But I would still urge someone to go there. Staying aware of your surroundings applies anywhere in the world. So, fearing something and respecting something are two different things. Be respectful and go and experience that mystical place and her people. If you *let* it happen ... be *receptive* ... it will change you forever.

Being There

In the last hours of April fools day 1999, I was driving to a local pub for a pint of Guinness when I drove up on some cars parked close together, with their headlights lit, on the other side of the road. In the median dividing the four-lane road was another car, stopped kind of crooked and unintentional. I could see the silhouettes of about fifteen people in front of the first car on the far side of the road. While I knew it was some kind of accident, not even the car in the median seemed to be damaged.

Just as I passed by it, I saw a man lying face down on the other side of the road. He was just in front of the silhouettes and this vision told the whole story:

The car that was now haphazardly parked in the median, had hit him.

What had taken me aback, was that no one was anywhere near the poor soul laying in the gravel and grass on the side of the road. At first, I thought that maybe he was dead and they knew it, so they were keeping their distance. But a strange instinct told me to do a U-turn and go to that guy ...

For whatever reason, it told me that he was *not* dead ...

That instinct proved correct ...

As I walked through the faceless people standing in front of the first car, I could see him lying there. He was taking short, deep, labored breaths. I bent over him and heard a gurgling sound. He was choking on fluid and in the lights of passing cars, I could see the thick, red puddle that his face was almost drowning in. I ran to my truck and retrieved a towel. After I wiped the bloody fluid away from his nose and mouth, his breathing eased and the gurgling stopped.

I looked at the people around me and I felt as though I was in a dream. They all seemed to be looking at the whole scenario as though it were on TV in their cozy little living rooms at home. For a moment, I felt a rage at these all too familiar "Rubberneckers". I just couldn't *believe* that these vultures had stopped and gotten out of their cars to look, and yet, not one had raised a finger to help!

But, when I looked back down at him as he took another breath, the rage went away as fast as it had came. I turned and bent over him and touched his bare, blood and scratch covered back with my fingertips. Every few seconds or so came another deep and yet short breath. They were almost like spasms, as though he were having to force his lungs to take the air.

I began to talk to him, even though I'm not sure why.

I just wanted to reach out to him somehow … to let him know some one cared.

As I spoke, I looked at his injuries and assessed that they were numerous and damaging. His left leg was a compound fracture and there were a lot of scrapes and scratches from his post-impact tumble down the road. But worst of all … was a large dented wound to the top, right rear of his shaved head. It wasn't bleeding very bad, but it was at least four inches wide and an inch or so deep. Another thing that shook me a little was his age … He looked to be in his late teens. *Maybe* his early twenty's at best. I thought it strange that he had been walking alone.

I spoke to him in a voice that I would use if I were speaking to a friend I had bumped into on the street and I told him to concentrate on the sound of my voice. I told him to hold on and to keep taking those breaths for me. I really believe that he could hear me because he seemed to be taking these heaving breaths more often. I promised him that if he could do that for me and not go to sleep until the ambulance arrived, he would be okay.

He stopped taking them for a moment, my lips closed together and my breathing stopped for a moment as well. I bent down over him and when I put my fingertips on his back again, he took another breath. I started talking to him again and assured him that I was still here. I again asked him not to go to sleep on me, because he was going to be alright.

Just then, I could hear the ambulance coming up the road. As I spoke again, I could *hear* the excitement in my own voice.

"You hear that my brother?" I said. "You're home free … just don't stop taking those breaths for me. I know it's hard, but they're almost here and you're gonna make it, I just know it."

He took a few more breaths, but just as the ambulance pulled up ... he stopped.

I know it's incredibly pretentious of me to assume the thoughts and feelings of another person, but I really felt like it was all that he could do to take those breaths for me …

For *him* …

But now that the ambulance was here, he felt that he could rest. My heart sank.

As the three rescue workers, two men and a woman, piled out of the van, I stepped away. The deputy, that had arrived only moments after I had, coerced everyone else to the back of the last car … but not me. He said not one word to me and I wondered if he had the same instinct about me being there as I had had when I first saw the poor fellow lying alone on the side of the road. I truly felt that I was supposed to be here and, it seemed, the deputy thought so too. When I looked at him, he gave a blank stare and turned to call the trauma 'copter on his radio.

The first EMT, who was now leaning over the pedestrian, stood up and yelled out "Has any one seen this guy breathing in the last few minutes?"

My heart sank even deeper as I told him, with all the urgency I could muster, that the pedestrian had been breathing right up to the moment when they pulled up. He nodded at me but didn't speak. The others were busy opening boxes of emergency gear and I don't think they heard me at all. When I looked back at the first one, he was kneeling down to join his co-workers examining the injured youth.

They looked at his wounds and, after they put on their rubber gloves, they rolled him over onto a backboard and then placed a foam collar around his neck. I watched as the third EMT put a set of electric paddles on his chest and I waited for the familiar jolt … but it never came. They looked and mumbled to each other and then removed the paddles without even giving it a try.

I wanted so badly to scream out "Go for it Dude! If he's gone, what have you got to lose?"

But … the words were just not there.

The situation had overwhelmed me …

Again … I felt like I was dreaming.

They put the backboard onto a gurney and lifted it up so that the wheel assembly fell with a loud squeak to the ground. For the first time, I could see the pedestrian's whole face … I was amazed to see that his eyes were now open.

He seemed to be staring, with a peaceful smirk, into the cool, star filled sky and I wondered if he could see or hear anything at all. I looked out in the direction of his stare, but all I could see was the dark outline of the trees on the side of the road … and stars.

I watched the second EMT, a woman in her mid-twenties, turn towards the deputy as the other two lifted the gurney into the back of the ambulance. Her face was expressionless, though it seemed to me that she working very hard to hide her emotion. Her eyes were wide and she never blinked as she spoke. Perhaps she was new, I thought. The deputy didn't seem to notice, he never looked at her face. In a monotone voice, she told him not to bother with the 'copter …

"This one's code", she said.

For someone who's so full of emotion, I can't say that I've *ever* felt like I did at that moment. I looked at the deputy and he gave me the same blank stare that he had given me minutes before.

Without saying a word, I picked up my towel and my keys and I walked back to my truck.

My head hung in a daze … If this *was* a dream, it was a nightmare.

I threw the towel into my truck-box and climbed into the drivers seat. I held the ignition key in my hand and watched the ambulance pull away with its flashing lights on … but *no* siren. I sat there for a minute or two, trying to chase off the malaise that had overtaken me. When I finally did leave, I quickly caught up to the ambulance. Not that I was speeding really, but that the ambulance was in *no* hurry.

Through the rear windows of the large ambulance, I could see two of the EMT's sitting over him, talking. Their faces were somber and calm. As I turned on my street and headed home, I watched it drive on into the darkness. Its silence was painful. I'd forgotten all about the beer. When I got home, I sat here at my computer desk and wrote this piece.

I don't imagine that I'll ever know why the pedestrian gave up his fight by the side of the road on that clear April night.

I know he was trying, I could *feel* it.

But I like to think that he heard my concern for him in those last few moments … that maybe he could feel it ... *and* … that he didn't die alone.

EPILOGUE

For the next thirty days, I called the morgue to see if I could find out the pedestrians name and then maybe get in touch with the his relatives. I'm not sure why I felt this compulsion, or even what I would have said to them, in such a horrible moment in their lives. I guess I just wanted them to know that somebody was there with him. Maybe, it would help ease their sorrow.

In those thirty days, I learned that he had no identification on him and, because no one had claimed the body, nobody knew who he was. As the thirtieth day approached, they actually asked me if I wanted to try and claim the body for burial since I was the only person who had shown any interest in the pedestrian ... I respectfully declined.

He was never identified … As far as I know, no one ever came to claim him.

This frustrated me as much as that fateful evening. I was told that he was cremated at the Pasco County Animal Control incinerator and buried out near Dade City as a "John Doe".

After reading this, my dear, close friend Michelle asked me if I thought I might be an Angel. She had recently read a book that said that they roam the earth and do not even know or realize they are Angels. But ... they are sent to places and moments in time, to help people through things.

I was so taken aback, I couldn't even answer her. I tried to shrug off the question with a joking quip ...

"You *do* realize who you are asking that, don't you?"

She smiled and let it pass ...

Thank goodness.

I mean ...

What on earth do you say to a question like that?

I had been accused of being, even *called*, the Devil *many, many* times in my life, but *never* an Angel!

(Yet Another) Pirate Looks At Forty

"Mother, Mother Ocean ... I have heard you call.
I wanted to sail on your blue waters ... Since I was three feet tall.
You've seen it all ... You've seen it all ...
-Jimmy Buffet

I've always loved that song ... "A Pirate Looks At Forty". Of course when I first heard it, I was rolling-skating my teen heart out, my sweaty palm nervously holding the hand of some girl for a "couples-only skate", stumbling through the words so that I wouldn't have to look her in the eye. I probably looked pretty silly singing about turning forty when I had only recently got my restricted drivers license.

I've never forgotten that girl ... and I have never forgotten about that song. I guess I was a romantic, even in those days ... Even if I was still shy around girls. My romanticism has blossomed into the full-blown hopeless type ... and my shyness has become almost legendary gregariousness (Okay. at least *locally*, anyhow!)

But in these last few days ... The last days of my thirties ... I've seen that song in a slightly different light. I always did understand, in a way, what he was singing about.

From the first day my Grandpa took out into the Gulf of Mexico when I was six years old *and* (Ironically) about three feet tall, I've been fascinated with the ocean. I've always loved pirate movies and any and all things adventurous. If you've read anything in my non-fiction catalog, or know anything about me, you know I am quite thee adventurer. I've never climbed Mount Everest, or swam the English Channel ... But I have had a *very interesting* life so far. I have seen and done things that many people will never have the chance to do. I have been to places and met people that would fascinate even the most jaded jet-setter.

I have shaken the hand of some very influential people ... Let's see, How 'bout Richard Nixon and Hubert Humphrey ... They were campaigning for the oval office in the late sixties, my Grandma was a reporter for the local paper in Aliquippa, Pennsylvania when she brought me to the shopping center where they made a speech on their campaign trail. I think I was five or so, maybe younger.

I also met Colin Powell; he was speaking at some big corporate motivational show being held at the Orlando arena. I was working the show as a stage hand and while we waited out back for the show to be over so that we could tear it down and load it out, he came out to his awaiting motorcade. We were just outside the door and he smiled at us as he realized who we all were. (Probably a little disconcerting ... Hell, *rattling* even, to be a man in his position and exit a building into a crowd of ruff looking long-hair types, all dressed in black and staring at HIM!)

Well, let me tell you ... His eyes went across us once and with a grin, he immediately accessed us for who we were. Now you'd think a man who has ran armies, consulted Presidents and helped to change or at least write, history ...

A man who just got paid some ungodly sum of money to give a speech to a bunch of conventioneers who were probably more interested in the after-meeting events in the hotel bar than his speech, a man who had his own police escort for crying out loud ... Would nod and whisk himself into waiting limo and the non-confrontation bliss afforded the man of his stature ...

Not on your life!

He stopped, calm as any moment I'd ever seen him on TV and he asked us how we were all doing. He waived off one of his body guard-types (probably secret service) and shook some of our hands. He made eye contact with all of us and seemed strangely eager to talk to us. While he did, he politely asked us how our day was! Can you just imagine?

He was as personable as any true gentleman I'd ever met. (Benny Hinn, Rod Stewart and a few others I've worked for as a stage hand, don't even want to *see* the local crews when they come and go, let alone seem to *want* to have a chat with any or all of them!)

Mr. Powell didn't look down at us, he smiled *with us!*

He shook a few of our hands and I am proud to say mine was one of them. It was raining, his "People" told him they'd have to hurry if they were going to make the airport in time with the wet roads and all. I am a great judge of character (most of the time), I swear, he was disappointed that he couldn't finish shaking *all our hands* … you could *see* it in his face. He reluctantly, almost frustratingly, agreed with the men in black and bid us a good day. We all wished him well too, and then headed in out of the rain to start our load out.

The disappointed look on his face never left my mind that day … Or, for that matter, to this day …

I wondered if he was somehow lonely in his world … Missing the camaraderie of old "chums".

A world constantly choking in protocols and being "politically correct".

A world where your eminence front is surely carving a shape of it's own into the face you were born with.

A uniformed world so full of rules that you grow weary of worrying if you've said or done the wrong thing … and to *whom*, constantly watching your step, as well as your words … Always having to second guess yourself as well as most of the cutthroat types you often deal with in a world like his. A place where you wake up in the morning and get handed a schedule of what you are going to do today … and worse still, where you are going to go today.

Not a life … An itinerary.

Just imagine being a man of his stature … Yet, some one else told you when and where you were going to eat! Everyone in your world … there to do a job. No one there to be a real friend … It makes my free spirit shudder … A very lonely world.

I wondered if chatting with "the guys" was a much needed respite from his prison.

After all, this was a man who had spent many decades in the camaraderie of the Army.

In a war zone, you *exist* with *real* friends. Those friendships are as real as they come.

A prison I doubt he saw coming … We rarely see the walls we build until the morning we wake up and discover that we can't see over them.

A lonely place indeed, for a man as real as he seemed to be to me. Funny, we Americans often chide and make jokes about how fake our Presidents and other politicians are and have been …

Makes you wonder why he refused to run for that oval office … doesn't it?

I haven't voted in all my life, my view on politics and politicians is bleak at best … If that man ever runs for President, I will register to vote and I will vote for him.

He was "real". Not only important these days … but *rare* as well.

Of course, working in the production industry, I've also met and worked with a lot of stars. I've been a spotlight operator for many famous artists … from Mel Torme' to Tina Turner … During Super Bowl 35 at Tampa's new Raymond James Stadium, I was the spotlight trained on Steven Tyler and Brittany Spears as they sang "Walk This Way" during the halftime show. So, if you watched it, you've seen me work …

Small world, huh?

As a lighting director, I've met countless stars; my fingers have been the board operator or moving light programmer for countless more. Blood, Sweat and Tears, The Fugee's, Snap!, Bone, Thugs and Harmony, Method Man and Red man, Onyx, Etta James, Eryca Badu, The Lords of Acid, Digital Underground (*with Humpty*), Ms. Rita Marley (A sweetheart), her son Ziggy and the Melody makers as well as several other members of their family, not to mention almost every other Reggae artist you could think of (and a few you probably haven't heard of yet).

I was the Lighting Director for "Sting '96"; a Reggae festival held every year on Boxing Day, in Kingston, Jamaica. At this particular show there was a special guest, Biggie Smalls … Sadly, it was to be one of his last shows. I remember he was in a wheel chair.

On a lighter note, there's a Funny story behind that show … I had been the L.D. for the Def Jam 10th Anniversary tour. One of the main DJ's for the show, (He spun for Meth & Red) was a very cool guy called "DJ Enuff". He and I got to be good friends as the tour progressed, because I too, had been a DJ for more than a decade before that. (More on *that*, some other time).

Before the tour ended, he had given me one of his shirts, it had his personal logo on it and I wore it proudly. (My hand to God, I'm wearing it RIGHT NOW!) Well, as I stood on that stage in Kingston … Christmas day, 1996 … wearing this shirt, tweaking some moving lights that I had positioned on the stage … I heard a familiar voice call out: "Nice shirt."

I looked up … And there he was, I hadn't seen him in over a year … Not since I'd left Manhattan. Neither of us knew that the other would be here … and lo' and behold, I was wearing his shirt!

Small world, funny story.

One more?

If you insist …

How 'bout this one? I never *dreamed* while I was roller skating, that one day I'd actually be onstage with Jimmy Buffet … But it happened! On his "Carnival" Tour, they needed four different looking stagehands to dress up in colorful costumes and dance around during the opening of the show and then collect the curtain when it fell … I was one of those guys at the Ice Palace show in Tampa …

Onstage with Jimmy Buffet! (There are Parrot Heads out there that would drown you in a keg of spiced rum for a chance to do that gig!) Where you there? If so, then once again, you've seen me work … Small world.

My life is *full* of those kinds of stories. I usually write in sadness because it's therapeutic, instead of about all these wild and crazy things that have blessed me. (I gotta work on that one!) Where I'm going here is that even though I've had some unbelievable moments … I've always been restless …

"Okay, I've done this … What's next?"

I know it makes me sound ungrateful … Believe me, I'm not.

It's just that I'm always trying to see and do and learn …

I am hopelessly in love with experience … And inner expression.

"Yes I am a Pirate, two-hundred years too late …
The cannons don't thunder, there's nothin' to plunder …
I'm an over-forty victim of fate …
Arriving too late …
Arriving too late."

I think you are getting the picture though … I've been living a sometimes-amazing life. I wouldn't trade what I've experienced for anything. But if you think these things I've done so far are lofty, you should try and picture some of my earlier goals in life …

I wanted to be a fighter pilot …

A Test Pilot …

An Airline Pilot …

Hell … *any* kind of pilot … And still loftier than that, I had designs on becoming an Astronaut!

When that all went the way of the winds, I was singing in a band, (For all *that* was worth … I was terrible!) So I wanted to be a rock star! If you ask, you'll find, most DJ's are disgruntled musicians … I was no exception. But by doing that, first in radio, then in nightclubs, began a journey that took me all over the world as I got into doing concert lighting by learning moving lights in the nightclubs.

I was in the proverbial right place at the right time. The moving lights were still relatively new to the concert industry, so my being adept at them made a valuable crewman rather quickly. The band brought me something else though that I didn't realize until almost two decades later … Writing! Back then, I only wrote song lyrics and poems, but once I started to write stories, a floodgate opened and out came *all this STUFF!*

Fiction … Short Stories and a whole novel!

My own, albeit different, brand of Philosophy …

More Poetry …

And the ideas for many more stories …

Why Me?

Who knows … ?

I don't fight it, I learned a long time ago to just go along with things … (Okay, *most* of the time, anyway!)

And so this searcher now has yet another, seemingly impossible, aspiration … Being a writer. I say "seemingly impossible" because I have no schooling at this whatsoever … I graduated from High School (Go Cobras!), doing only half-decent in English. I did and always have though, loved to read.

I think that between my love of a good story and my fascination with studying and understanding people, I have found something new that I could be good at. I've always had an artistic side … and, without really seeing it, I've always done some form of work that let my creativity vent.

Herein the philosophy …

Everything happens for a reason, whether you understand it, or not.

Learning to recognize it may *never come* … but trust me …

Learning to accept it will *always* make things easier …

Well, I'm too old to be a nightclub jock any more.

You eventually get to dislike the new music … A sign from the universe that it's time to quit. Besides … the age difference between you and the crowd also begins to show itself … no matter how young you *feel*. It's not that you feel old … it's that you actually begin to see how young they are as compared to you and your friends. What amuses them, quite often does *not* amuse you …

I'm getting too beat up to keep doing the grueling, and sometimes dangerous, local concert production work. *This* comes in the signs of limping, memory loss and shear dislike of teaching someone else your gig so that they can later *steal* it from you …

The Army wouldn't take me as a helicopter pilot at 18, I doubt they'll have me now ... and let's face it ... becoming an Astronaut is completely out of the question ...

And I *still* can't sing ...

> *"Mother, Mother Ocean ...*
> *After all the years I've found ...*
> *My occupational hazard is ...*
> *My occupation's just not around ...*
> *Feel like I've drowned ...*
> *But I won't wear a frown.*
> *Yes, I feel like I've drowned ...*
> *Gonna head up town."*

Ol' Jimmy ends this song in a satirical, kind of joking, up-beat note. An acceptance of his life that can only come with the wisdom of age. On a later live album, he says he wrote this for "a friend", but I wonder if bits of it were *actually* about him. (Did I say album? God, now I *am* showing my age!)

I like to end most of my philosophical essays in a similar way. That's the therapy of writing. You not only divulge your innermost thoughts ... You get to come to terms with them as well.

Do you think I got this from him?

Do you think that he'd think I stole it?

Nah ... Pirates always shared their plunders!

Written one day after my @$#*ing Fortieth Birthday!

Summer of Love

"Sometimes at night, I see their faces ...
I feel the traces ... they've left on my soul.
And those are the memories ... that make me a wealthy soul.
I tell ya those are the memories ... That make me a wealthy soul."

~Bob Seger. From the Bob Seger and the Silver Bullet Band
title: "Travelin' Man"

It was the summer of 1980 and I'd just got off the phone with Alicia. She was now up in Detroit with her Mom. Even though she had been gone only a few weeks, it felt like years. It was the summer before my junior year in High School and I was hating every minute of it. I missed her like I couldn't believe.

I first saw her one fall morning, when she boarded our school bus. In my small community of Moon Lake, Florida, everyone knew everyone. How could this vision of beauty ... this Angel with long blonde hair and a smile that could blind you ... be hidden around here without my knowing? You see, I lived on this side of Pasco County for a long time. I knew everyone and everyone knew me. But she appeared out of nowhere. I'm sure this mystery intrigued me as much as her beauty. My buddy, Larry, nodded up towards the front of the bus as she came up the steps and turned into the isle.

When you lived here ... you had very close friends ... and talking without talking comes as second nature when you're that tight. When I saw her, I almost died. She was just so different from all the girls that I was used to being around (Not that I lived around a bunch of ugly girls, it's just that there was something different about her). She was drop dead gorgeous, Well, at least to me she was. I've always been attracted to the "Girl next door" type.

Larry got up and gave her his seat and at first I thought ..."What a dog!" But he didn't think fast enough, as now she was sitting next to me and her head was at my level! I got as nervous as I could possibly be ... Then I asked her what her name was and where she was from. I'm sure I did so with little quips and jokes because I was quite the jokester in school and I remember her smile beaming at me as she answered. She told me how her and her ex-boyfriend had gotten into trouble at school and whatnot. Her parents sent her down here to live with her Grandma so that she could finish the last three years of high school, only going home during the summer.

I knew her Uncles and her Aunt. They had been in school with me for years. But we didn't hang out too much so I had never heard of 'Lisha, or about her coming to stay for the school year. The mystery was solved. But now it was time for an adventure! I had THEE most unbelievable crush on her you could ever imagine.

And we hadn't even gotten to school yet!

She was in my grade, but she had none of my classes. That was no problem; in my school most of the staff liked me a lot and in turn, I got away with a lot. I could wrangle up a hall pass or get permission to go and "Thread a film" for another teacher almost at will. Don't get me wrong … It wasn't that I was a bad kid. I was just say … Very mischievous!

I went to the guidance office and, from my friend who was a student aide there, I got all of her info. What classes she had, her full name, her former address, school records … everything!

It was good to be the King!

The next time I got to chat with her I was at a party where there was a live band. I was just learning to drink so I was passed out in front of the right side of the bands sound system. Everyone thought that was so cool! "He must be wasted to be laying there!" they all giggled …

Did I mention that the band was PLAYING?

At any rate, she saw me and laughed/admired with the rest. After about an hour, I woke up (Read: Came to) and went in search of more beer. It was a keg party and the keg was outside. I got my beer and went towards my car to check on the stereo system. Hey … You just never know at these kind of party's.

Well lo and behold, who do you think was sitting on my trunk?

My Angel!

I wondered if she knew it was my car since another of my best buds, Shane, was jammin' the tunes for her on my Pioneer Supertuner. Led Zeppelin Live, I believe it was. I approached (Read: Staggered over to) her out of the darkness and she turned and jumped when she realized I was right beside her, cool as a cucumber.

I looked at her, smiled, and without saying a word, pounded one of the two beers I was carrying. (I needed the free arm to hold myself steady.)

She spoke to me and I felt a fuzzy quiver that I had never felt before. She asked if I was feeling better after my "Nap" and if I had a cigarette. I gave her a butt and lit it for her. She steadied my hand with hers as I lit it and the way she touched me sent me straight to Nirvana.

I tried like mad to get her to sit in my car and listen to the stereo with me ... But she had seen that movie before. I finally gave up and settled for chatting with her on my hood. That was prophetic, as we would later come to spend a lot of time on that hood and in that car, listening to the stereo.

She asked me about myself and if I had a girlfriend. I told her I had just gotten rid of one (Funny, I don't remember her name) and that on no uncertain terms I was the KING at our school! She looked at me sarcastically and said that she had already noticed that everyone knew who I was and that they all had some funny story about me and my buds' crazy antics. (Like the time I rode my motorcycle through the school chasing a teacher that had earlier smacked my face unjustly!)

"But being notorious doesn't make you the "KING" Jeff Gaines!" she spouted. I stood up and turned in front of her. She sat back, not sure of what I was gonna do. I relished in that moment with a pause ... then shot back with; "Is that so Miss Alicia Dawn Kersey, 10922 Gerald Martin Road, Livonia, Michigan?" I had studied her records over and over again that day and my reply floored her. The stunned look on her face was priceless.

She said "Oh my God ... How could you know that?" I waited with an evil stare and then looked her in the eyes and told her; "Like I said, I'M the KING!"

I stuck out my tongue and headed back to the keg without asking if she wanted another beer. (I was gonna bring her one anyway.)

"Let her chew on that for a while" I thought.

But it was me who was to end up chewing ... when I got back just in time to see her getting into a car to go home. Her Grandpa was very strict and they were almost late. I pounded both beers and went inside to lay back down in front of the band's sound system.

Her Grandpa didn't allow visitors, especially men, so the only time I could see her was at school or if she could get away, chaperoned, of course, by one of her Uncles or her Aunt, to the beach on Moon Lake. I lived on the lake right up the street from the park and I would go there with my buds every day.

One day at school I asked if she could come over and study with me and somehow she got permission to do so. I don't remember the whole plan, but it was probably something sneaky. After we had finished studying, I asked her if she wanted to go hang out at my neighbor's house and she said yes. My friend Larry had already asked her out and she had turned him down ...

But something about the way she smiled at me when she saw me told me to ask her ...

We went across the street and started up the three steps to my neighbor's door. Before she knocked, I stumbled through something to the effect of; if she wouldn't go out with Larry, then maybe she should go out with me.

She stood on the step above me and smiled as she said, " It's about time ..."

My heart was goin' a million miles an hour ... An adrenaline junky since I was a child, this was the maddest rush that I'd ever had. " ... I was wonderin' when you were gonna get around to that!" and with that, she bent over and kissed me.

It was one of the sweetest kisses I can ever remember.

Just then, my neighbor opened the door and knocked us off his trailer's stoop and into the grass on our butts. We looked at each other, my angel and I, laughing at our first kiss.

When she smiled into my eyes at that moment, something clicked in me so hard that I swore she and my neighbor could hear it!

We spent that school year bonding at an unbelievable rate, considering how little time we could share together. My mom was flabbergasted at the way I was so cheerily going to school every day. In the evenings, Alicia would sneak out or get permission to go to the store for a Pepsi. She would call and I would make the run to the store in about a minute and a half ... Did I mention that the store was a mile and a half from my house?

She could hear the tires on my '72 Chevy Nova singin' as I raced down the curving country roads to be by her side for only a moment. On one such trip, we were on the side of the store. She was sitting on the hood of the old green Nova and I was standing between her knees trying to get in kisses as she talked.

She told me that she had a lot on her mind and somewhere in her voice I could tell something was up. She looked up at me and said; "You know … You're really are easy to love. You do everything so right. When I'm in a bad mood you just ignore it and go about your business. You always make me smile and …"

I interrupted with; "What are you trying to say sweetheart?"

You see, I really wanted to get in some kisses before I had to drop her off at the end of her street. I wasn't really needing any compliments; she always made me feel secure in our relationship. But what she said next rocked my very foundation …

She looked me in the eyes and this smile was one I hadn't seen before.

She said: "Jeffrey Jay Gaines … I love you."

My mouth fell open … I had an uncontrollable tear in my eye.

No girl had ever said that to me before. At least not in way that made me feel it!

In *that* very moment in time …

I realized what love for a girl was, and that, I was VERY much in love with this one!

I looked back at her and smiled a smile that was new to me as well …

"I love you too." Was all that I could muster.

We hugged each other tighter than ever before. It seemed to last forever.

I will never forget that moment as long as I live.

At the time of this writing, I've only felt that love for a handful of women. It would seem though, that I've never learned to see love sneaking up on me like that. It's happened several times since.

When I kissed her as she got out of the car that day, I noticed that our kisses weren't the same. After that they never were. They were better. I guess kissing the one you love is always better. Over the next couple months our petting got more and more passionate. Nothing sexual though.

It wasn't about that, this love we shared, it was pure. Pure as the young hearts that were nurturing it.

We were both 16 and I could not stop thinking about how this girl could be my wife! I saw us together forever. That's how you think when you're 16 … and in love. Nothing is more important in the whole world and should it stop spinning while you two were together, that would be fine.

My bud Louie and his girl Kim went with us to Walt Disney World one weekend. She lied to her grandparents that she was staying at Kim's house for the night and we snuck off to a motel on Colonial Blvd. in O-town. The next day, we spent ourselves out while exploring the park, we had the time of our lives!

We were young, in love and we ruled the world for those moments!

She slept under my arm in the car on the way home and when I dropped her off that night, I knew it was going to be a LONG summer without her. You see; she had to go home and spend the summer with her family in Michigan and then come back in the fall to return to school.

I went, along with her Grandma and her Aunt, to drop her off at the airport. Her Grandma was cool and she knew what was up. I was fine through the whole trip. But when we got on the escalator to go back to the main terminal, I began to cry. I didn't mean to. But the thought of not seeing her tomorrow … let alone a whole summer, just body-slammed me.

Here I was, big, sports playin', fist fightin', country boy tough guy … bawlin' like a little baby. In front of her Grandma and Aunt to boot!

I couldn't believe their response … They were crying too!

Not for her … FOR ME!

I wasn't ready for that. They looked at me with their lower lips out and rubbed my back with reassurance. They made me promises about how the summer would pass quickly and that she'd be back before I knew it.

I wiped the tears from my cheeks and mumbled something about having something in my eye …

But when I look back now, I know they didn't buy it for a minute. I didn't say a word in the car on the way home and they let me have my silence.

I woke up the next day with a knot in my stomach. And so began my summer. My Stepfather and I got along like vinegar and soda mostly. He could never understand a boy so full of play. His childhood, it seemed, was not exactly fun. I couldn't understand how any one person could be so obsessed with work. And so our relationship went, He & I, incessantly fighting about when to work and when to play.

I had just gotten off the phone with her (Remember the phone?) and I wasn't ready for the loud, threatening, tongue lashing I was about to get. It seemed I hadn't done the lawn when HE wanted it done. I was told that I wasn't going to get my allowance 'till it was done. It was Friday and I had planned to leave on a camping (Read: PARTY) trip in about an hour.

He and my Mom were leaving, they would be gone for the evening and now I had NO money for my trip. Even if I mowed it NOW! I was furious! I thought about Alisha and the hopeless situation of my home life. It was one of those frustrating moments that make a teenager scream.

I stormed into the house, put a few changes of clothes in my well-stocked backpack, found $17.00 or so in change and called my friend Louie. I had just gotten the last of the change from the bottom of one of my Moms purses when his Dad dropped him off at my house.

My next adventure was about to begin …

I had Louie drive me out state road 52 to The ol' Dixie Highway … I walked into the Chevron station that is now a huge Flying J truck stop and spoke to the guy under the car on the lift. I asked him for a piece of paper and something to write with.

He gave me an empty cardboard soda flat and a piece of yellow tire chalk. I made a the sign on the hood of my Nova, right there where I discovered love …

It read simply: "DETROIT OR BUST!"

I thought it was short and to the point. Louis gave me a big hug and I swore he was going to cry when I got out of the car. I walked up the northbound on-ramp onto the shoulder of the acceleration lane of Interstate 75, set my backpack down and I propped the sign up against it. I put my headphones on and hit the play button on my Walkman cassette.

Bob Seger filled my ears …"*Up with the sun, gone with the wind, she always said I was lazy. Leavin' my home, leavin' my friends. Runnin' when things get too crazy … yeah … Out to the road … out 'neath the stars … feelin' the breeze … passin' the cars …*"

That song, "Travelin' Man" and the one right after it, "Beautiful Loser", fit that summer to a tee. Louis had turned me on to that record and his passion for it told me it was good. Alicia, being from the Motor City just like Bob Seger, loved it as well. I bought "Live Bullet" on cassette so I could listen to it in my car with her and on my Walkman anywhere else.

I never could have imagined how well it would help me see my feelings. A lot of music does that for me. I love the way it lets you vent. A kindred spirit with the musician. I listened to the words and felt warm at how I was relating my adventure with the music. I stuck out my thumb and smiled at the next pack of passing cars.

My first ride was uneventful, a couple, going to Gainesville. They were nice though, and they offered me something to drink. I got out at their exit and as soon as I stuck out my thumb, a car pulled over. I ran up and asked where he was headed to. He said he could take me to Atlanta. That would put me there at about 3 a.m. I figured. I could pitch my tent beside the road and get a fresh start in the morning. I smiled and hopped into the car.

His name was Ted, I think, I'm horrible at names. He was black, about 5'10, wearing a cowboy hat and smoking a cigar. He was out on leave from the Army base he was stationed at. He had to be back by morning, so he was in quite a rush. That was fine by me. He was getting me closer to Alicia with every car he passed. He was very cool and he couldn't believe a young white boy like me was groovin' on B.B. King. It seemed I knew the words to most of the songs on his tape. Man, did I blow his mind when I pulled my own B.B. King cassette out of my backpack!

We bonded over the next few hours and I was really happy to make him my friend. He listened to my story and admired me for my courage. He couldn't believe I was only 17. I loved listening to his stories about the Army and he loved listening to my Bob Seger tape.

About an hour over the Georgia State line, his car engine began to smoke.

He had let it run low on oil …

We had just spun a bearing … and thrown a rod. (Look it up, it's bad, believe me!) He looked at me and shrugged his shoulders. I did the same and, without saying a word, we both started to take our gear out of the car. I figured he probably felt like I had no obligation to stay and help him. (I would though. My Mom definitely raised me to have a conscience and to be considerate of others. He had stopped to help me and now I had the opportunity to show him my concern.)

I knew the car was dead and he had to be at that base by 0700 the next morning. I smiled when I realized we were already so tight we could talk without talking.

He told me, after an hour of unsuccessful thumbing, that he wanted me to keep trying and that he was going to go try and use the phone to call his Sergeant. I fussed a little when he wouldn't let me go with him, then watched as he disappeared up the on-ramp.

When I look back now, I realize that he felt we weren't getting rides because he was black. That's why he wanted to leave me alone to hitchhike. When he didn't come back in an hour, I walked up to the little gas station to find him. He was surprised to see me and he stammered a little on what he was trying to say to me.

He told me to go back to the road and keep trying. He told me a lie about his Sergeant sending someone to get him, but that failed when I told him I would wait to catch a ride with him too. I told him we could keep each other company, and that I wasn't too keen on leaving him alone here in a place that he had already told me he felt uncomfortable in.

(This was, after all, the Deep South.)

He was my friend and I was going to show him just what you get when you befriend me. I take that *very* serious.

He shook his head at the no win situation.

I knew he was lying.

He knew I knew it and I wasn't going to leave him there alone.

He looked at the ground and chuckled, then put his arm around me and told me; "You alright, ya know-it?

We smiled at each other and I patted him on the back.

We picked up his gear and headed back down the on-ramp to the highway.

The old Chevy 4-door whipped off the highway with a squeal. We turned at each other and, without talking, grabbed our gear and ran to the car. Any good hitchhiker knows that you look inside the car and talk to the driver before you get in. You settle on how far each other are goin', then you decide if it's someone you want to ride with. It's a special instinct that you must follow carefully. Again, we worked together without talking to each other.

After the introductions, the driver stared at Ted and said that "He" could get in the back. The remark made me nervous, but it was late and we hadn't gotten a ride in hours. As we cruised up the road, the driver got more and more drunk … and his driving got worse and worse.

He began to get a little belligerent about how "normally" he would " … NEVER pick up a Nigger a hitchhikin'!" I sat with my back to the front passenger door and winked at Ted. I never took my eyes off of the driver … or my hand off my double-edged boot knife. I couldn't believe that he used that "N-word" right to Ted's face! He was getting weirder with every drink from his flask and I was actually beginning to worrying about whether we were gonna survive this guy or not. My heart was racing.

I thought about my Mom … I thought about Alicia … my life back home …

When he took a route around Atlanta to the west, and he refused to stop and let Ted out, we started to panic. Ted needed to get out here (Me too, for THAT matter!) and go northeast on 275 to get to his base in South Carolina. (I just wanted out!) I started to think out a move on the guy and Ted grabbed my arm from behind the seat.

Ted gave me a look that said "No!" and I went with his silent suggestion. The driver said he knew a better route on the north side of Atlanta and he'd let Ted out there.

The car weaved on …

About 20 or 30 miles above Atlanta, the drunk noticed we needed fuel again. I was so relieved. The tightness of my chest was about to kill me. When we pulled into the truck stop in Adairsville, Georgia, I was even more relieved to see the cop parked by the gas pumps.

There would be no scenario, we were gonna walk away from this nut and watch him drive off into oblivion. I remember looking up into the clear night sky and silently thanking God.

The drunk looked at us and told us to stay put as he went to pay for his gas. Right on cue … without talking, we waited 'till he was in the truck stop, then grabbed our gear and piled out of the car. We walked over to the cop car and as we did, Ted told me that the drunk had showed him a small revolver when we stopped for gas the last time.

I wonder to this day, just where that situation would have went had I tried to bully the drunk into stopping. We told the cop about what had just happened and how the guy was drunk and that he had a gun. The cop watched him evil eye us as he pumped his gas.

Then, when he left, the cop pulled him over. After a while, the cop came back and said that he was letting the driver "sleep it off" in the back of the truck stop parking lot …

He also said that he found no gun.

The cop was beginning to remind me of the drunk more and more every minute. I really felt like the way the cop was acting towards us changed when Ted said that he was in the Army.

It was like he became nicer … but, it also seemed like a nuisance to him … He had started out with a demeanor like *we* were the bad guys.

Ted and I didn't have to talk about that either. He could see that I was truly beginning to understand his world. I saw it in his eyes as he saw my perplexing look turn into one of surprise. In that truck stop parking lot, at that moment, I saw the world, as a whole, in a brand new light. Before that, I'd never realized just how deep racism ran in this country. I'd also just *experienced* it, first-hand.

We asked the cop how much cab fare was back to Atlanta, and he said it was 20 dollars or so. Ted said that he had that much, so we called a cab and went back to the Greyhound terminal downtown.

At that time, the government would pay for any GI's transportation to an awaiting duty, so Ted would soon be on his way.

He told me that he wasn't going to let me try and make it alone, so he walked me up to the window and he asked how much a ticket to Detroit was. When she told him, his head bowed in defeat. He didn't have that much. I thought quickly and told her that I had a cousin in Fort Wayne.

She punched some keys on her pad and came back with a smaller figure. His head rose with a smile and he replied triumphantly; "We'll take it." She told me we'd have to hurry though, as the bus I needed to be on, departed in 20 minutes. Ted's bus wouldn't leave for 2 hours.

He grabbed me a hot dog and a Pepsi on the pretense of going to the bathroom, and then walked me to my bus. Just before I got on, he gave me his Cowboy hat. It was brown leather and he pulled the long, frilly feather out of it, then pushed it down on my head.

"Heeer Partna', this looks a lot better on you big man." He said, straightening it just so.

Before the driver put my pack under the bus, I had given Ted the Bob Seger tape. I told him that I could get another and I wanted him to have it for his car. I told him he didn't need to give me the hat and he pushed it down even further. I re-adjusted it as the Bus driver told me, "Sir, get on, or off, the bus ... We have a schedule to keep." I gave him a scowl and shook Ted's hand for the last time.

I hadn't even sat down when I realized that we hadn't exchanged numbers or anything ... I looked in the mirror at the snobby driver. I knew getting him to stop was a lost cause.

Ted and I waved at each other and then I watched him watch the bus until we turned the corner towards the highway. I was so sad to be on that Greyhound ... at that moment ... and I would give anything to buy that man a beer right now.

It's funny how a few short hours and a little bit of adversity can bring strangers so closely together … I wonder about him often.

The trip to Fort Wayne was uneventful. I arrived at about three-fifteen in the morning. My cousin Skip was pretty miffed that he had to drive all the way across town in the middle of the night to come and get me. He put me to bed with a lecture about running away from home and scaring my Mom like that. I told him I had called her collect twice since I had been gone.

I told him about how impossible life with my stepdad was. But he said I should take it like a man and not be doin' such "childish things." I didn't even go into the Alicia part … Remember Alicia?

Well, when I got up the next day I reread her love letters for the bazillionth time, then I got up my nerve and I called her. I was blown away that she didn't know about my current adventure and that she thought I was still in Moon Lake!

(There wasn't such a thing as Caller Id then!)

I envisioned me hitchhiking up there and hiding in the woods on the 3 vacant lots across the street from her house. She had described them to me once, so I knew they were there. I thought it would be so cool to wait for her to walk down the street and then sneak up behind her and cover her eyes …

I could just imagine that smile that so filled my heart with joy. She was gonna freak out that I was actually THERE … Right there with her! I loved her and if this didn't prove it … nothing would!

That smile she wore was for me. It was because of me.

This girl loved ME!

I remember feeling at ease as I went to bed that night. I couldn't wait to put my plan into action the next morning. Tomorrow, I thought … "I'm going to be with my 'Lisha!"

It only took me two rides to get to Livonia. One guy took me north on 69, and the next guy took me east all the way into the city.

I was trembling as I pitched my bright orange tent and camouflaged it in the woods across the street from her house. I needed to get my backpack and stuff out of the rain and I didn't want anyone to see me … Namely her. I was only 200 feet from the house that I had heard so much about while we bonded on the hood of my Nova.

I was still shaking.

The hat Ted had given me was keeping my face dry from the rain and I wondered where he was and if he was doin' okay. I wondered what he did about his car. I wondered if he had made his muster that morning. I wondered if his friends made fun of him for listening to Bob Seger.

I watched as it started to rain even harder. I thought that it was stupid of me to think that she would be walking down the road anytime soon in this downpour.

I took off my shirt and hat and climbed into my tent.

I must have been tired … or maybe it was the rain, but I fell asleep …

I awoke to the sounds of kids at play. They were playing Army and I was still young enough to remember the sounds of that game. I climbed out of my tent and into the cool Michigan drizzle. I looked around at the kids who were surprised to see that I was right here amongst them and they hadn't even detected me!

They thought I was really cool and they asked me if I wanted to play Army with them … I declined. I was proud of my camouflage job.

Then … I turned and looked at someone coming down the sidewalk!

My heart was racing … It was her!

And Donald …

The guy she had supposedly been broken up with all this time …

They were holding hands, laughing and smiling, skipping through puddles down the street in the rain like I didn't exist!

When I left on this adventure, I was the "Travelin' Man" … and now … I was the "Beautiful Loser".

I sang the words in my head ... *"Beautiful Loser ... Read it on the wall ... 'cause it's easier ... and faster when you fall ... you just don't need it all ... ahhh ah ... you just don't need it ... All!"*

She wore the same smile for him ... that I had hoped to see for me.

I was alone.

I was 17 years old ... and on the noblest mission of my life.

I was over 1000 miles from my home ...

From Louie and Shane and Larry ... My Life.

I felt the entire world cave in on me. There wasn't a breath in my soul.

I wondered if she would have come back to me in the fall and pretended that everything was all right. I wondered if I just hitchhiked home right now, could I pretend that I didn't know?

Could I have her for just one more school year?

I know these thoughts were silly ... But you think like that when you're 17 ... and in love.

It was at that moment ... that I learned about women.

It was at that moment ... that I learned about love.

It was that summer that I became a man.

If she was my first true love ... then this was my first true broken heart.

Not even Ted's cowboy hat could keep my face dry.

This piece is a non-fiction essay that is my personal coming-of-age story, telling the tale of my running away from home and hitchhiking across America at 17, for my first Love. But after reading it through the first time, I realized it was so much more than that and that I had learned so much more about life ...

And about the world I lived in ... especially its people ... than just about Love or becoming a man.

"Perhaps travel cannot prevent bigotry, but by demonstrating that all peoples cry, laugh, eat, worry, and die, it can introduce the idea that if we try and understand each other, we may even become friends."

~Maya Angelou

After posting this on Hello Poetry, I had *SO* many messages asking what happened after that.

I admit ... it does indeed end abruptly. But I did that to amplify to the reader the emotion of going through all of that struggle only to discover what I did. I wanted to leave the reader with that very emotion as it was *such* a turning point ... such an epiphany ... such a life-changing lesson in my life. It was a feeling that I have never had since. One that I think some may never have had ... *and* ... that many *have* had.

Well, I won't do that to you beyond here. I think you've gotten the picture. What happened afterwards, was this: I went to her house to ask to use the phone so that I could call my parents and ask for a a plane or bus ticket home. I obviously had nothing to keep me here. But, her Mother was having NONE of that! She got on the phone with my Mom and these two loving hens conspired to *keep* me there ALL summer!

And so ... I did just that. Her brother was my age and we paled around having a great time, going to keg party's, swimming in the Boxford Township pool and so on. I got a job, bought a 10 speed ... and just spent my summer in Livonia. I even went and spent a weekend with some other friends I had known in Junior High that had moved back to Monroe, Michigan.

It was a good time, for sure. Her Mom was such a sweetheart and she didn't want me going back home all bitter *and* back to the turmoil that I guess my Mom had clued her in on.

Alicia and I even got back together briefly, *years* later. But, I think that it was just us both not wanting the "ending" to be the way it was. Perhaps, to prove to ourselves, and each other, that the love we shared as teenager's, all those years ago, was real. This "demonstration" as-it-were, worked, *but* ... it also taught us that you can rarely, if ever, go back. The past is usually just that ... the past.

We parted quite amicably a midst realizing these things and even had a laugh about it all in hindsight. After all, we were still kids back in those days. Kids becoming adults ... but kids, just the same. Amazing kids ... that both became amazing adults. Free spirits always have the greatest adventures. We remain good friends to this day. She's a wonderful gal that will always hold a very special place in my heart.

Hedonism, Perseverance

and the Life of a Pair of Blue Jeans

"I've seen things you people wouldn't believe ...
Attack ships on fire off the shoulder of Orion ...
I watched C-beams glitter in the dark near the Tannhauser gate.
All those ... moments ... will be lost ...
in time ... like ... tears ... in the rain."

~Rutger Hauer as Roy Batty
From the Ridley Scott feature film "Blade Runner".

Hey, got an old pair of jeans that are just your favorite ones in the whole world? You know, the ones that you either have, or would, hide from your significant other so as to keep them from being tossed into the garbage, or worse still, the Salvation Army bag? (Perish the thought of someone else *ever* wearing your beloved memories!) Well, when you quit grinning with your fondness for that ol' pair of jeans, go and put them on.

Yep, right now.

Go On!

I want you to be wearing them while you read this. If you've since cut them into cut-offs, well then all the better! Go on now, put 'em on! If they don't fit quite like they used to, just leave 'em unbuttoned. I won't tell a soul.

I promise ... I swear.

We both know the only reason they're a little tight right now is because you've not worn them in a while and everybody knows cotton shrinks with time. Huge Thanksgiving dinners and beer-swilling Labor Day weekends have *nothing* to do with it whatsoever!

Right?

Comfy?

Great, let's roll! I wanted you to put those on for a bunch of reasons. Firstly, for that smile on your face. Are you lovin' it, or what? I know why you smile dear reader and it's not just because you're comfortable. That leads to my second reason for the quick change. It's that strange ability of those jeans to parody a microchip. A chip that store's some of your fondest, most endearing memories.

One that stirs up some of your innermost emotions.

You *love* these pantaloons ... They mean the world to you.

You cherish them and the memories they hold, both visible *and* invisible.

Like the holes in the knees for instance, battle scars from sliding across the grass that summer playing Frisbee. (Not only a care-free fashion statement, but great in the "surprise breeze" department as well!) The pinky-red transmission fluid stain from the time you took a road trip and found yourself playing the role of shade tree mechanic in the middle of nowhere. (Remember when *all* gas stations had garage bays and honest mechanics? If not, ask someone born pre-1975. It was a better time, indeed.)

We can't forget the frayed pockets either. A waiving reminder of every dollar you persevered to put into those pockets *and* every one that you eagerly pulled out and tossed to the winds of hedonism. Oh, and we have to mention the crotch-seam patches and re-sewn belt loops so lovingly tended to by a grandmother or sweet old tailor lady that you entrusted to mend your beloved duds.

Remember the day you got them? Whether you found them under your Christmas Tree or hunted them down as a skilled shopper at the mall, you knew you loved them as soon as you pulled them on. They were a much darker indigo and just a little stiff. Tight in some places and loose in others, still as yet uneducated in the unique form of your lower extremities.

The first few times you wore them, they pinched, bit and chafed you. You found yourself tugging and adjusting them endlessly until that one glorious day when they popped out of the dryer or off of the line and slid over you like a custom made skin.

They made you feel good when you wore them.

They boosted your ego when you gazed at yourself gracing a mirror somewhere.

They pumped you full of confidence each and every time you caught some fine example of the opposite sex checking you out as you walked through the pub or club or maybe even the mall where you two first met. ("It's gotta be the jeans!" You thought.)

By now though, they weren't just jeans, they were actually a part of you.

You found yourself sometimes washing them twice a week so that you could wear them more often. At first, you wore them kind of like dress pants. Nice shirts or sweaters along with new shoes of any color; all harmonizing with them to make an ensemble that made your statement. *Only* the blue found in blue jeans can so effortlessly match *any* color.

Strangely, almost sadly, the inevitable life cycle of ol' Levi Strauss' wonderful creation was underway. The more you wore them, the more comfortable they became. The more comfortable you were in them, the more you *wanted* to wear them.

The more you wore them, the more you had to wash them … the paradox of their existence.

As their life progressed, they silently changed appearance, gallantly fading with each spin cycle and stoically bearing the scars of carrying their owner through life's trials and tribulations.

Eventually, you replaced them as "Dress" jeans with a new pair, but your love of these jeans was stronger than ever. You just couldn't wear them to a nice restaurant or out on a blind date, lest you be looked upon as a person who was not fashionably sensitive. (Read: You dress like a bum!) Not to worry, they still had many days of usefulness to be had while out with your buds or camping at your favorite spot.

Always perfect for errands or trips to the store. Shoot, they'd probably even work on your second date for that matter.

Then that dreaded day came …

The day when your adventures finally left a scar that would make the fashionably sensitive types turn up their noses in disgust. A scar, in the form of a tear or a stain, that couldn't be overlooked. Alas, the day of retirement from "anytime" jeans had arrived.

Sure, you tried to *sneak* them out at night. But inevitably, someone made a comment or an outright crack about their state of wear. It would seem *they* didn't feel you were being politically correct in your choice of garments for that particular event. (Probably just jealous of you for being so comfortable.) Your second skins had finally crossed the line into that netherworld. You know the one. The one that slated them to being worn only on *your* time. No devil-may-care attitude on earth could now disguise their battle scars.

After all, who could possibly be turned on by that dingy yellow mustard stain on the front thigh? Yup, the one that not even half a bottle of Shout could get out. That one you got when you almost rear-ended that guy while you tried to mow down a burger on your way to the Carnival. (Who can afford a burger at the Carnival?) You didn't even *care* who saw it as you strutted down the midway; as far as anyone knew, it was simply a medal for having so much fun on your favorite ride!

It was a badge proudly worn the whole day through. All the places you could no longer wear them to went racing through your mind as you scrubbed … and soaked … and pleaded with the stain.

Your prayer for it to at least fade … spoken in silent desperation to the laundry Gods.

All that scrubbing …

All that *living* …

All that sacred and precious time spent in your favorite old friends. You taught them how to fit you like a glove. You showed them off and you showed off in them. You not only washed them, I'll bet that you had a special spot just for them in your drawer or closet, didn't you? In return, they made you feel like a star! They protected you from the mosquitoes before you got the bonfire up and blazing. They saved your legs that time you slipped in the grocery store parking lot. They kept you warm that night you left the theater and the temperature had fallen twenty degrees. They felt like part of you whenever you wore them.

They *were* part of you even when you didn't. Going through so much together had formed a bond without measure. They were part of the family!

Funny thing, that bond between us and a pair of jeans. Funnier still is how we ourselves are like a pair of jeans. We come into this world shiny and new. We are rough around the edges but everyone loves us. Without trying, we can be annoying because we require a bit of attention and even more patience. As we grow older, we begin to take our destined form. We fearlessly face work and play with equal bravado. We work hard to be able to enjoy ourselves as often as possible.

By and by, all that work and all that play eventually take their toll. We start to fade, some more apparently than others. When we are young, our material thick, dark and new ... we are loved and accepted by all. Adored by the elderly and accepted by our peers.

As we begin to fade, showing the scars of life, our look changes and we find that the younger people start to treat us a little differently ...

We're not as "cool" anymore.

Hero to zero, in just ten dryer cycles.

Most of the elderly treat us with distrust and many of our peers try to be indifferent, lest they expose a weakness or, Heaven forbid, they let us know that they are jealous.

During that fade from dark indigo to sky blue, we find that we aren't accepted at all the places we had been only a few years before. We discover many of our peers are so concerned with gaining every else's approval that they will *never* give us theirs.

Then comes that inevitable day, when we, like our beloved jeans, are just too old to be accepted by everybody. Not even the faded jeans feel comfortable around us.

We have become cut-offs ... the final stage in our life cycle. Oddly, we also might be at our most comfortable. Sure, we sometimes long to be un-faded and tight. But then we realize how uncomfortable that really was sometimes ... how awkward some of those moments were.

Then we start to reminisce about those sky-blue days. Those days when we were the coolest and the world was our oyster. The cut-offs envied us. The stiff newbies looked up to us, often emulating our style or our actions. As we bask in the glow of those memories, we also remember all the scars that came with those experiences. The thought of those lessons brings us back to reality.

This is the way it's *supposed* to be.

We, like our beloved jeans, have done our job. We have lived our lives. We didn't see anything coming … we just did our thing. Our life cycle was always underway from the start, elegantly fading as we grew through our peak season. Now, we can only hope that our efforts have earned the love and respect of someone who will cherish us in our last days as cut offs.

Before we knew it, all that experience …

All that hedonism …

All that perseverance …

All that *life* … had taken its toll on our appearance.

The heart was still there. The soul was still there. More importantly, all those memories were still there. But, when you've been reduced to a pair of cut-offs, it's hard to find adoration from even our closest friends and family … Let alone, total strangers.

I think there's a lot to be learned here, from these faithful old blue jeans. I think maybe we should see ourselves in that very light we shine upon them …

We know they're a bit tattered.

We know they're a bit torn.

The fading of the material is beyond evident.

The stains and patches, our medals of experience, stand out against the sky blue skin we love with all our hearts. We should each realize that *we* … are all we have. Everything else is incidental. If only we could love ourselves like we love those old jeans, I think it'd make facing our golden years (and the *rest* of our lives for that matter!) a lot easier.

It might even make us look at cut offs with a newfound respect and dark new indigo with a little more patience. Where we are in our cycle is not in our control. So, passing judgment on someone who's in a different stage than ourselves is really a futile waste of energy.

When I was in my early twenty's and just beginning my "broken in" phase, I went to pick up my girlfriend from her job at a nursing home. She was running behind that day because they were short handed. I wandered inside to see what was keeping her. While I sat in the day-room waiting for her, I struck up a conversation with a gentleman in a wheelchair. I was wearing a Civil Air Patrol t-shirt and soon we were chatting away about airplanes. To my amazement, he was not only a retired fighter and airline pilot, but he had served in *both* World Wars.

As he spoke, I couldn't take my eyes off of his hands or his eyes. As I listened to his stories about dogfights and being taken prisoner in Germany after being shot down … By mistake … by one of our own bombers in bad weather; I found myself hypnotized by the thought of all the things those hands had touched or built or fixed in his eighty-odd years on this planet.

I was spellbound trying to even attempt imagining all of the things his glassy, faded eyes had seen. I was completely overwhelmed by these notions. This old pair of cut-offs before me had seen, done, learned and lived things that could fill pages and pages with truly amazing adventure. His life cycle had been simply extraordinary!

Still, here he was …

Like our old faded friends we barely, if ever, wear anymore …

Sitting quietly in a drawer somewhere …

Waiting for his final chapter …

An amazing collection of memories …

A collage of his interactions with mankind …

The endless echoes of an exceptional lifetime …

An entire *collection* of laughter, sadness, learning, travel, love, pain, tatters, tears, frays and stains … the well-earned badges of somebody's hero. I'm sure many relished in his accomplishments.

But now. these well earned medals lie hidden in plain sight, barely, if ever, noticed by the busy nurses and doctors who were here to look after him until he was passed on to that great Salvation Army drop-off center in the sky.

See how alike we truly are … All of us and our favorite old Blue Jeans? We relish in someone or some thing until it can no longer serve us. We pamper, patch and coddle as long as it's a means by which to preserve something near and dear to us.

But as soon as it's more trouble than we're ready to deal with, we let go and move on. The love is still there, but it would seem we've turned off the emotion that usually goes along with it, like a switch. We won't "wear" them for fear of embarrassment or the possibility of confrontation. We fear disapproval. But inside, we cling to our fierce allegiance to them.

Why do we hide it then?

Isn't that what *true* allegiance is all about?

Doesn't this expose a sad truth about ourselves?

Is it natural, or is it fear of non-acceptance disguised as conformity?

No matter which … it's *very* sad.

That day changed something inside me forever. I left there with a view of my own mortality I think few youths ever get to behold. I think of him and that hour we spent together to this day. You see, I went back the next afternoon to bring him some Flying magazines I had laying around my house. He had complained of the predictable boredom at the nursing home and I thought they might cheer him up or at least let this wise old pair of denims wander away from that dreary place for a few precious moments.

My heart was broken when I was told by my girlfriend that he had passed away in his sleep that very night. I sat in the chair where I had met him and I read through the magazines I had brought for him, his tales replaying in my mind. His eyes and his hands, all the things they had done and seen, gone forever.

My sense of that loss numbed me to my very soul.

I *so* wanted to look into his eyes again.

I *so* wanted to study his hands again.

The very contemplation of the life he had led was mind-boggling. When I left there, my girlfriend asked me what was wrong. I couldn't explain even if I'd wanted to. This was an epiphany for me … and me alone.

Wherever he is, I hope he's flying … high and free.

I hope his eyes shine bright and clear once more.

I hope his hands are busy and content. But most of all … I hope his jeans are soft and that they fit him like a glove.

Are you still comfy dear Reader?

Good.

Are you still lovin' those jeans … or are they cut offs now?

Better still.

Not to worry, I'm sure there was no love lost when you started washing your car with those snipped-off pant legs.

It doesn't matter.

What does matter is that you have *lived* in those jeans. You have had some great times together … you and those denims. You watched each others back and you looked *good!*

I hope that reading this made you feel even closer to them *and* to yourself. But more so, to those people around you that you love. As you can hopefully see, you aren't that different from each other … you, the ones you love *or* those comfy jeans. I also hope that this will help you to keep a better eye on your own life cycle. Remember, you can't stop or control it.

All you are allowed to do is persevere.

And *sometimes* … you get to partake in a little hedonism.

But no matter what happens, they fade with every wash …

With every experience …

Just like *you*.

Take care not to be too brutal on yourself *or* your jeans. Try and be more tolerant of other jeans too, no matter what cycle they seem to be in and never … *ever* … loose touch with just where you are at in that cycle …

You *or* those sacred Blue Jeans.

Girls From Other Realms

"You're dangerous 'cause you're honest.
You're dangerous, 'cause you don't know what you want.
Well you left my heart empty as a vacant lot
For any spirit to haunt.

You're an accident waiting to happen.
You're a piece of glass left there on the beach.
Well, you tell me things I know you're not supposed to
Then you leave me just out of reach."

~Larry Mullin Jr. ~Bono ~Adam Clayton ~The Edge
From the U2 title: "Who's Gonna Ride Your Wild Horses?"

My Best Friend

The best Friend I ever had was a beautiful mare. She had the most gorgeous, huge brown eyes with little green flecks all through them, and the most beautiful long black mane you've ever seen. She jumped over the fence from my neighbor's yard one-day and, according to the law, she was then mine. I have no idea why she did this, but when she pushed her head into my chest with an adoration that could only be compared to my adoration for her, I knew it was to be.

It was the happiest day of my life. You see I had never dreamed she would be mine. I saw her every day and never gave her much thought except that she was young, seemed to be very bright, and had just enough attitude to make her intriguing. But never did it cross my mind that she and I could bond.

Every day I would wake up and look upon her with a joy that could not be measured. She was everything I ever wanted in a horse and then some. She knew just when to walk. She knew just when to run. And she never let me get lost. We spent our time roaming through fields covered in wildflowers and sometimes we would watch the sun set over the mountains on the edge of my mind.

She listened intently to my banter of useless information and all my old war stories like a contented pupil in a class with a teacher she had a crush on. I adored her. Never in my life had I found such peace and contentment. And every day I would look at her and wonder just what I had done to make her jump that fence.

When we came home from our adventures I would brush her down and comb her mane and tail, it gave me so much joy to just look at her and touch her and smell her. Everything about her was like a dream, and I often thought I was going to wake up to find it was just that. Everything she did made me smile and when she sensed that something was troubling me she had an uncanny ability to make everything all right.

No one in the world ever made me feel the thoughts and emotions she seemed to pull out of me without effort. I told her things about myself that I had never shared with anyone. And the time we spent together meant more to me than anything in world. She was my best friend and I loved her more than life itself.

But one day she jumped back over the fence and, according to the law, she was my neighbor's horse once again. I tried for a moment to coax her back to me, but the light in her eyes was gone. It was the saddest day of my life. I watched her run and prance in his pasture and she seemed to be happy.

But I couldn't watch her because my heart was broken. It seemed like forever since I'd been out in my backyard because I don't want to see her, and I don't want her to see me. I never felt so lost and alone in my whole life. And though she didn't know it, every once in a while I would look out my back window at her just to see that she was safe and content. I think and wonder and worry about her constantly.

Then one evening I heard her braying really loud at my back fence and instinctively without a thought ran out to see her. The look in her eyes was one I had never seen before. She seemed confused and maybe a little sad. Without any words, her eyes said she missed me but she could not jump the fence. I thought about cutting it but that would be against the law. Just then I saw my neighbor leave on his weekly jaunt into town. And I climbed the fence and mounted my mare. All night we explored all the places we used to go to. It was my birthday and never had I been given such a present. It was the best birthday I ever had.

When we returned I brushed her down and combed her mane. The smell of her was intoxicating and as I looked into her eyes I swore I could see that light still burning in the distance. I adored her for a long last moment then jumped the fence and went into my house without looking back. My neighbor was due home any minute. I've never been so confused in my whole life.

I'm going to start saving my money today. I'm going to see if he'll sell her back to me.

You know what they say though … Some things money just can't buy.

This is my first-ever short story. It is a fictional metaphor about real events in a relationship ... The horse of course, representing a girl that I was very much in love with. During our split, we both had a very hard time staying away from each other. There was an extreme passion in our feelings for each other. But ... she had some very deep and serious issues from her past that made her do things that constantly damaged our relationship. Issues too personal and involved to explain here.

I tried everything to urge her to get help about it, but she just refused to follow through with it. After long months of this futile effort, I had to walk away. But that proved far and away harder than I ever imagined ... for *both* of us. I wrote this after she had left my cottage on one of our last trysts. She had dropped by in the middle of the night.

That is the symbolism of jumping the fence. It was either/both of us crossing that "line" drawn when you are supposed to be finished with a relationship. She had stopped by after a point where I had thought we were finally finished. Confusion, when dealing with her, was constant. That is not to say that I wasn't guilty of "popping" in on her either. Mea Culpa. It was all so very sad. I have never been in love like that again.

I realize the innuendo of the "riding" the horse. Believe me, that was not my intention. I didn't even realize it until I had read through a few times. It almost made me not show it to anyone. But after a while, I did ...

I just never explained that the story was a metaphor. Most folks humored me and told me what a nice story about a horse it was ... or ask me if I ever did get the horse back. Funnier still, some asked me where I kept and rode my horse. I would just explain that it happened long ago and let it rest.

It is also why I never posted it on Hello Poetry. I didn't even want to have that conversation or have folks make the innuendo observation and then have to see it posted under my story in the comments. If you, dear Reader wish to accuse me of penning subliminal erotica, then have at it. I'm mostly over the whole thing and you can feel free to give it any Freudian analyzation you wish.

I simply wanted to share it here because it was my first non-fiction essay. Not the first that I would write about a girl in my life ... To maintain their privacy, I found it better to use metaphor.

Swim

I was snorkeling one afternoon in the often-murky waters of my hometown. The visibility was as hazy as ever. I swam among the usual schools of fish and took care to avoid the Sharks, Barracudas and little Prickly-fish that can be so annoying if they brush against you. As I swam over the top of my favorite reef, A most beautiful light caught my eye …

In the murk, I couldn't see what it was emanating from … but without a thought, my fins pushed me   straight towards it. Gliding over the flat grassy bottom between the reef and the shore my heart began to race in disbelief …

There …

Swimming just under the waves …

Looking at me …

Was a Mermaid …

When you stop laughing, I want you to picture how I felt. I couldn't believe it, and I knew no one else would either. But my fascination wasn't the fact that she was a Mermaid at all … I was awestruck by the light that shined all around her.

It was amazing. It wasn't any one color … It was all colors … and no color at all. Its radiance and sparkle were absolutely captivating. I couldn't look away from it even if I had wanted to … And I didn't want to. If she had turned out to be some kind of ocean going huntress in search of her next meal, I would have easily been her next victim. I would have willingly done anything to be shown in that breathtaking light.

Lucky for me she was harmless … at least physically. I had to remind myself to take breaths as I tried to get closer without scaring her away … Like I said, she was looking at me too. The light continued to lure me … I was held there, completely helpless, in its grasp. As I gazed into it, I couldn't figure out where it was coming from.

At first, I thought it was her smile. Then I thought it might be from her eyes …

But I was wrong on both counts …

The light was coming from her …

I could feel it around me like a warm breeze on a balmy Florida night.

I wanted to stay there …

Forever …

Forever in that moment of seeing this wondrous spectacle for the first time. But time is persistent and often cruel. And the moment left me. I was distracted by shadows that appeared in the light as I got closer. My emotions swirled like an eddy in a tidal pool as I realized what the shadows were … Her light had attracted many other swimmers and as I looked at their faces I could see that they had been attracted to the light, just like me.

I didn't know whether to be jealous or feel sorry for them … after all, I still didn't know her intentions. I watched them staring into the light … I knew how they felt … But in that moment I also felt what they wanted. I began to recognize some of them as Sharks, Barracudas and Prickly-fish …

Part of me wanted to chase them off … To defend and protect her. But I am a live and let live type of person. Besides, out here in the ocean, if you let your guard down to save someone … you might just find yourself as the meal instead. I chose to keep my distance and watch her. But to my overjoyed amazement, she spoke to me. I didn't understand her language, nor she, mine. But we were able to communicate enough to begin some kind of bond. It was all I could hope for. It was all so quixotic.

That first encounter ended all too soon. After all, I couldn't stay in her world for long … and, I would soon find out, she couldn't stay in mine. Everyday I would return to that area near the reef. I couldn't help myself. I could see her light even when I closed my eyes … it had, for those first few days become part of me. Its grip was warm and welcome.

With each visit I tried with all my might to teach her my language and to learn hers. There were many moments when the frustration from lack of understanding pushed us apart. But, I was so enamored with her, that I not only braved the Sharks, Barracuda and Prickly-fish, I went and got my license to scuba dive so that I could spend more time in her world.

She seemed to appreciate my efforts, but the first few times I tried to bring her to my world, She changed her mind or something drew her back to the sea. I would walk up on to the beach and turn to see her reaction to its beauty, but she was gone. I wanted to hold her hand as I swam towards the shore but I'm not like that. I needed to know that she wanted to come to my world. That was important to me and I felt like maybe that would help her understand me better … More frustration.

One evening on the third or fourth try, I found myself alone in the surf again. I was convinced by this time that she didn't want to come to my world. She always seemed appreciative of my coming to hers and even eager to come to mine … but each time, I walked up onto the beach alone. I walked along in the sand that night … My head slightly hanging. I didn't know whether to be mad or frustrated. Our communication hadn't improved much in those first few weeks.

I turned to look at the Moon, as it set, big and orange into the ocean. I looked across the waves for her light but it wasn't there. Sadly I closed my eyes as I tried to think of what I should do … And there it was … The light … it washed over my face with a smile … her smile … my smile …

I wanted to let it go, but I couldn't. I stood there for what seemed like forever and basked in its warmth. But the thought, or maybe the realization that she was never going to come to my world, made me open my eyes … And, the moment left me … briefly …

To my amazement, there she was. She had walked up out of the surf while my eyes were closed. I looked at her and for a second I thought the light was gone. I was wrong …

It wasn't gone …

It had become my light too … or maybe she had finally let me stand inside it with her … I'm not sure to this day which. Those few precious hours with her in my world meant more to me than I could ever say. The look in her eyes and the way we communicated that night made me feel incredible. She shared so many things about herself; her world and her life with me that I felt honored and even privileged to be enlightened with such insight about her.

I found myself effortlessly sharing some of my innermost thoughts and emotions with her as well. By the time the sun came up, she was curled up under my arm as we slept on the floor. I was sure when we awoke that she would have to return to her world … but to my amazement she actually asked to spend more time with me! I was overjoyed.

There are those that have said that too much of a good thing is bad. Even a hedonist like me can agree with that. But I would have given anything to have more of those moments with her.

They were incredible.

They were without inhibitions …

They were without tension …

They were without stress …

But more than anything … They were without motive.

We were two glorious beings … both quite different … Both quite the same … sharing a few timeless moments together; neither wanting any more than a deeper knowledge of the other.

It was beautiful.

But perhaps it was too much for her … being out of her world for too long. She had told me she'd not left it in a very long time. I was glad to help her come out of her shell and look inward on herself a little. She had done the same for me whether she realized it or not.

But let's face it, my world can be a little overwhelming sometimes and I think she had had the proverbial "Too much of a good thing".

She almost seemed to panic. Her mood was one of aloofness and anxiety. Her statements started to become irrational and I found myself feeling not only frustrated … but also guilty. I was asking too much for her to spend so much time with me.

I know … It was She who had asked for the extension of our meeting. But I should have said no and let it end on a good note. After all … Time is persistent.

I had all the time in the world ... or so I thought. But, like I said earlier, I would have given anything to make those few moments last forever.

She was wonderful. It turns out that those were our last moments.

I took her to the beach and watched her as she waded back into her world. I begged her to let me come back to the ocean with her but she refused. Something I'd said or done had made her think that I now had a motive of some sort. I couldn't convince her otherwise. I tried, but it was futile.

I watched her slip under the waves and she was gone ... And so was her light. I was so confused ... I didn't know whether to be relieved or hurt ... blessed or angry. After a few nights, her light returned in the form of her siren calls from deep beneath the waves ... I would lay in my bed late, late at night and listen to them.

They were confusing at first, but when I realized she was hearing me as well, I became at peace with the whole thing. I was thankful for those few precious moments and sad to think that our inability to understand each other had pushed us so far back into our own worlds.

I guess there's some comfort in knowing though ... that time is persistent.

I think of her often.

To say that I've had some bad luck with women would be quite the understatement.

Obviously, this is a metaphorical story about a girl that touched my life. As I started to fall for her ... and her for me ... I began to realize that she was an alcoholic and she began to realize that I was not. I wanted to help her, but she wasn't ready for that, I guess. To try and explain it all here would turn this from a short story into a novel!

So, read between the lines, ponder it deeply, read into it it any way you wish. I simply hope that you enjoyed it.

Versus

ver·sus

ˈvərsəs,ˈvərsəz/

preposition
preposition: **versus**

1. against (especially in sports and legal use) or to struggle against.
"Penn versus Princeton"

2. as opposed to; in contrast to.
"weighing the pros and cons of organic versus inorganic produce"

Origin: Late Middle English: from a medieval Latin use of Latin : *versus* 'toward.'

noun
Second/further literal translations from Latin as a noun: **versus:**
line, verse, rhyme

"It is okay to be at a place of struggle. Struggle is just another word for growth. Even the most evolved beings find themselves in a place of struggle now and then. In fact, struggle is a sure sign to them that they are expanding; it is their indication of real and important progress. The only one who doesn't struggle is the one who doesn't grow. So if you are struggling right now, see it as a terrific sign — celebrate your struggle."

~Neal Donald Walsch

A Few From The Porch

"We can't plan life. All we can do is be available for it."

~Lauryn Hill

Dragonfly Love

As I stood on the porch this morning,
Listening to the birds
and taking in the sounds and smells of a new day,
I saw two pairs of Dragonflies.

They were each flying around one another
in an almost reckless dance.

Suddenly, one pair came together and tumbled briefly downward before flying
off together in passionate, Dragonfly bliss.

But the colorless female from the other pair, just as suddenly, broke off her
dance. She flew away … Leaving the bright blue male to land on a car antenna …
alone.

I looked at him,
almost motionless,
in the early morning breeze,
his body,
slowly teetering
with his wings.

I could almost feel
his sadness …
or maybe
it was mine.

But as I watched him
fly off
in search
of another dance
I swear …
I knew
how he felt.

At the time I wrote this, I was still living with a girl I was broken up with. We'd been together for nearly 5 years and I guess neither of us wanted to leave our bed. We had both been seeing other people on "dates", but would return home each night to crawl back up into that bed. It was likely the most absurd thing I'd ever been an accomplice to.

Mea Culpa.

We had both been seeing people we had met at our jobs. But, only three days before I had experienced this moment on my porch, the girl I was seeing had someone whisper a lie in her ear ... So, she dumped me and ran away; the truth not being exposed until it was just too late. But my ex actually ended up marrying her new beau a few years later.

On the morning I witnessed this, I was astonished. These 4 Dragonflies were mimicking the situation in my life at that very moment! We had both found someone ... but mine had flown away. I read somewhere that some folks believe that Dragonflies are "Messengers" of sorts. If that is true, then these were just plain poking fun at me.

Ya gotta laugh.

The Coin

I was sipping my coffee
on the porch this morning
and I watched a little boy
that was coming down the street.

He was dragging behind him
two plastic lawn chairs,
stacked one-on-top-of the other.

By the bitter, pained look on his face, it seemed
as though he was hating his task immensely.

He stopped down there,
right in front of my porch.
Yet, he didn't even notice me up here.

His eyes were fixated on a small, silver coin in his path.

He let go of the chairs with the abandonment
found only in a child tossing an old toy aside for a new.
He bent down and picked up the coin,
then rubbed it with his thumb.

It was too far away for me to tell its denomination.

After looking at it closely, he stuck it in his pocket …
His face was now beaming as he first looked up into the sky
and then back down and around in search of his chairs.

He picked them up and began dragging them off again.

But now …

So help me …

Accompanying his new-found grin,
was a noticeable, bouncing joy in his step.

I wish … we could all find a coin like that.

Witnessing this moment in time, gave me a "chin up" epiphany at a really sad period in my life. It showed me that even something really simple like that could, and would, eventually bring me back to "Happy".

And something did ... eventually. I've since learned to eagerly look for these things when I am sad. I swear ... It works!

I have to say ... I shared that little boy's smile when I went back inside to drop this piece on my computer. Knowing what I did with ALL my change at his age ... be it found in the couch, on the ground or even cashed-in pop bottles ... I often pictured him putting his candy and change on the counter at the local 7-11.

That too, made me smile.

BTW ... it is *indeed* the same porch where I witnessed the Dragonflies ...

Crazy what you see when you aren't "looking" ... Huh?

More importantly ... crazy what it can show you too.

The Universe is truly mystical.

A Few Lullabies

"Music is the one art we all have inside. We may not be able to play an instrument, but we can sing along or clap or tap our feet. Have you ever seen a baby bouncing up and down in the crib in time to some music? When you think of it, some of that baby's first messages from his or her parents may have been lullabies, or at least the music of their speaking voices. All of us have had the experience of hearing a tune from childhood and having that melody evoke a memory or a feeling. The music we hear early on tends to stay with us all our lives."

~Fred Rogers

"A successful song comes to sing itself inside the listener. It is cellular and seismic, a wave coalescing in the mind and in the flesh. There is a message outside and a message inside, and those messages are the same, like the pat and thud of two heartbeats, one within you, one surrounding. The message of the lullaby is that it's okay to dim the eyes for a time, to lose sight of yourself as you sleep and as you grow: if you drift, it says, you'll drift ashore: if you fall, you will fall into place."

~Kevin Brockmeie

Maybe I'm a Dreamer

Maybe I'm a dreamer.
Oh babe I guess it's true.
But, all I ever do Dear …
is dream … dream of you.

Maybe I'm a dreamer.
I guess it's a fact.
But, when I get to where I'm dreamin' of …
I'm never comin' back.

And if you don't come with me Dear,
Then where will you be?
You'll still be a dreamer …
Just like me.

You can't live on wishes …
Yeah, that's the way it seems.
But how can anything come true …
if you don't have a dream?

Maybe I'm a dreamer.
Oh babe I guess it's true.
But, all I ever do Dear …
is dream … dream of you.

A man has a dream …
and he works so hard.
Then he dies in the middle of his life …
while mowin' his yard.

Not me Baby … I want to live!
Our life here is oh, so short … and it *never* forgives.

You can't live on wishes …
Yeah, that's the way it seems.
But how can anything come true …
if you don't have a dream?

Maybe I'm a dreamer … Oh babe I know it's true.
But, all I've ever done Dear …
is dream … dream of you.

I wrote this lullaby for my HS sweetheart after she came over to my house crying and was all upset that her family had just told her to leave me and to "Forget that dreamer!"

I sang it to her while she cried on my shoulder on the couch, the next time they came at her with one of these attacks. It became a ritual with them.

They *really* disliked me.

I can't say I blame them, in hindsight. I was yer typical parent's worst nightmare: Long hair, torn jeans, loud-crazy shirts/clothes, singing in a band, bouncer at a pool hall, big mean Doberman Pinscher, hot rod Firebird Formula with a loud stereo, big ol' party house with a pool ... you get the picture.

It was what it was. I was whom I was in those days. We all do what we do as youth. We also all, *most of us anyways*, grow up and out of those things ... *mostly*.

I Love You

Do I ever let you down?
Have I ever made you cry?
I only want to make you smile …
Can't you see it in my eyes?

I love you
I love you, I do.
I love you
I love you, it's true.

Do I take too many chances?
Do I act like I got it made?
Well, if the sun should burn your heart …
can I please be your shade?

I love you
I love you, I do.
I love you
Honestly, it's true.

Do you see me when you're dreamin'?
Do you miss me when I'm gone?
If you can't share this love with me,
I guess I'll just move on …

But …

I love you
I love you, I do.
Every beat of my heart …
is beating for you.

I love you
I love you, I do.
With all of my soul …
I simply love you.

CLXIX

Another lullaby written for my HS sweetheart in the midst of our last falling-out. Sadly, I have since lost the melody. I wrote it one night after dropping her off in the middle of a fight and then sang it to her a few days later under a full moon, while slow dancing on one of favorite private beaches where we used to go and "park". Back in those days, these little gems dotted the west central Florida coast. Sadly, I bet you'd be hard pressed to find one these days.

We had been through so much in our 5 years together. Much of it growing pains and moments of self-discovery. Not to mention discoveries about each other. These things happen in your late teens and early 20's. But, as also happens, we also discovered things we didn't like about ourselves *or* each other. There is no doubt in my mind we were truly in love ... *deeply* in love.

But sometimes that isn't enough to make folks stay together when they have "issues", no matter what they are. It is a sad and undeniable fact. We pretty much tortured each other that last year or two ...

Neither wanting to stay in the relationship, recognizing its futility.

Neither wanting to lose the love they had not only worked so hard on, but that they believed in so much.

As humans, we aren't just conditioned to fight for something we believe in or care for intensely. It is in our very nature. No matter how bad it actually is for us, mentally or even physically.

Don't believe me? Ask *any* drug or alcohol or food addict ... *or* someone in love with an abusive partner.

We weren't abusive, in a physical sense ... but without realizing it then, I'm sure we emotionally abused each other quite a bit. Not in a mean, intentional way ... but by our selfish, still-too-young-to-"get it" actions. One of the life lessons often dealt to you in your youth.

This lullaby is the perfect example ... Here I was writing and singing these words for her in the midst of yet another of our endless fights ... and I meant them with all of my heart ... and yet, I really did just want it all to be over to stop the predictable and repeated fights and suffering. It happens every day and will for eternity. It is the stuff of songs ... of poetry ... and operas. Human nature is undoubtedly the most complex and confusing thing in the ever-known.

Dawn

You came into my life
like a beam of light.
A beam that would brighten
my dark, darkest night.

I'm sorry I didn't notice you,
but my eyes were still blind.
I'd just lost a love
and my will to find.

But like the sunrise
described by your name ...
you're beautiful ...
and I'd never be the same.

You picked up my heart,
caring and kind ...
without even asking ...
and you eased my mind.

To my surprise
it all seemed so right.
I tried to resist,
but I just couldn't fight.

Because like the sunrise
described by your name ...
you're beautiful.
I would never be the same.

You wrapped my heart with yours,
all my sorrows left so fast.
I began to hope beyond hope
that these moments would somehow last.

But you knew they never would,
for that was never in your plan.
Simply an Angel, earning her wings
come down to heal a man.

And like the sunrise
described by your name ...
you're beautiful.
I'll never be the same.

-Christmas Eve 1987

After five years together, and being engaged with her, my high school sweetheart and I split up. It was inevitable. We were kinda bad for one another anyways. Lies, cheating, etc. and far too young to really get what being married really meant. And even if we were finally realizing it, it was far and away too late. The damages were already done. It would have ended in tears, no matter what, I'm certain of it. Leopards rarely change their spots. The distrust of each other was fully manifested.

While in the "daze" of this split, I met a girl that was known, in my small town, as the most beautiful around. Everyone knew her, as she was a bartender at the hottest club in town and when guys spoke in circles of women in town ... they were inevitably compared to her.

I knew her in passing. she had made me many a drink. But I paid her little mind as I assumed someone of her caliber dated professional athletes or really rich guys. She was nice, as was I ... but that was it. Besides, in those moments ... back in those days ... I had a fiance.

I got a DJing gig at the after hours bottle club and lo-and-behold, guess who worked there? I was in such a daze, I still gave her barely a glance. This drove her mad, apparently. She asked the other bartender, an old friend of mine from school who had gotten me the gig, why I was so snobby. Her reply was to explain about my ex and I and that I was really tore up about it.

Being the Angel that I later learned she was, she decided to be my self-appointed rebound girl. You read that correctly. SELF APPOINTED! I swear, I wanted nothing to do with it. Like I say in the lullaby, I tried to resist. But she was having NONE of that. In those next several months, she was my constant, and I do mean constant, companion. Unless at work, she wouldn't let me be alone for a moment. I have to admit, while it sounds like crowding or choking, it wasn't ... and I didn't mind at all. She constantly made me laugh and smile.

None of the guys in town could believe she was my girlfriend ... and none would believe me when I swore we were "just dating", because we were seen all over town day and night ... Restaurants, Pubs, Pool Hall, Beach, the Mall, parties, slow dancing at the local Dance Clubs, the Go Cart Track, Denny's at 4 a.m. ... everywhere.

Being with her took all that soul crushing pain away. I was eating again. Laughing again. Holding my head up again. I wasn't drunk out of my mind every night. Even my thousand mile stare had disappeared. She made me happy and filled me with the cocky confidence I'd once wielded like boss. She was just a Godsend.

But towards the end, I began to really fall for her. She had told me that we would NEVER be boyfriend/girlfriend. THAT was how she convinced me that she wouldn't end up hurt as a rebound girl and to let her in.

But now, ironically, it was me in danger of being hurt. Angel that she is, she sensed this and gently let it end just after our big New Years "weekend".

I knew it was coming, we'd actually agreed to it being our last hurrah. But on Christmas Eve, I wrote this lullaby and I sang it to her in my waterbed, with a Santa cap on, as I held her in my big arms with her head on my chest. She cried a bit and squeezed me tighter than she'd ever done before.

It was my way of saying "Thank You ... and "Goodbye".

I was such a mess when she had scooped up my heart. I suffer to think of the downward spiral she never let me fall in to ... especially after I tried so hard to resist her in the name of chivalry.

In hindsight, it was HER who had given ME the lesson in chivalry.

She truly is an Angel.

(Anti)social Media

"The nature of your tragedy
Is chained around your neck
Do you lead or are you lead?
Are you sure that you don't care?

There are reasons here to give your life
And follow in your way
The passion lives to keep your faith
Though all are different, all are great

Climbing as we fall
We dare to hold on to our fate
And steal away our destiny
To catch ourselves
With quiet grace

Storey to storey
Building to building
Street to street
We pass each other on the stairs"

Andrew Farriss And Michael Hutchence
From the INXS title: "The Stairs"

(Anti)social Media

I guess I'm too intense.
I guess that I'm too nice.
People are so on guard these days
they return it in kind
with ice.

People have become so afraid
of other people.
I can't say I blame them at all.
But it's not just others they are afraid of …
They are afraid of dropping the ball.

Everyone is so judgmental.
Everyone out for themselves.
What does it say about us as a race
when we put others lives on shelves?

We seek "followers" and "likes"
just as if they were gold.
What happened to the friendship, kindness and generosity
we once shared in days of old?

"Look at my dress!"

"Look at my dinner!"

"You're such a loser …
And I'm such a winner!"

"I heard that his Dad don't have a job!"

"I heard she's too poor to come on spring break!"

Is this really who we have become?

We bask in bragging and showing off,
but to empathy we have become numb.

Why should I care about somebody dying
or relationships ending?
It's not my problem ...
"Oh look, I'm trending!"

Everyone is out there playing
one big video game.
It is destroying us and who we are
and nothing is quite the same.

And it's not just that this problem
is addiction systemic.
This nightmare of our age
has become epidemic!

We seek approval from those
who could actually care less.
We scold and scorn upon any perceived weakness
and only praise on success.

Its bullying enablement
brings children to kill
or to kill themselves
in a hopeless loss of will.

We outlaw drugs
when for fun we all use.
The same must be done
for this scourge and its societal abuse.

Glory and popularity have taken a whole new meaning
where, to have them we'll take things all too far.
We've lost sight of the forest because of the trees
and lost faith in just who we are.

Letting someone help you or you helping them
brings questions of motive and suspicion.
If we won't trust our friends and our family
how will higher consciousness ever come to fruition?

We upload and post our lives
into a new consciousness they call the "stream".
I know that pride cometh before a fall …
But what happens when we cease to dream?

I have never engaged in these practices.
I am way to private for that.
See, the friends that I have, have been there for decades
and they always have my back.

These little flat screens have become our alters
where we willingly offer our souls.
All in search of feeling better …
turning blind eyes to all of its brutal controls.

Smash them I say!

Ground them right under your feet!

I don't mean your phone … I'm using a metaphor …
for these soul-crushing apps that you must delete!

We must escape this death
driven by vanity.
Rise out of it all
and lose the insanity.

There's a great big world out there …

Go out in the sun!

Snap out of this hypnosis …

And go have some fun!

Stop staring at a screen

And KNOW that you LIVE!

Their judgments mean NOTHING!

You've PLENTY to give!

Leave that laptop behind

Get out of the house.

You just may find a real friend or even a spouse!

Talk with them … using your voice.
Listen to them … using your ears.
You just might find a kinship in a soul
that actually lasts through all of your years.

But above all else … feel this person
Relish in all the moments that you've seen.
Laugh with them, cry with them and always remember …
You will never get a hug from a screen.

Kinda speaks for itself.

For total transparency: I have a "MySpace" page ... somewhere. Haven't been there in years. I also have an Instagram page to post pictures for friends, fans and family. It is a convenience, not a lifestyle. I don't seek (or chase) followers or aspire to be an "Influencer".

Everyone I am following, I know personally. (With thee singular exception of Madonna. Hey, I was a DJ for 20 years. Her and DJ's have a very special relationship. So sue me or call me a hypocrite. It's not like her and I chat it up on the weekends.)

It is also not about my ego. I NEVER did FB or ANY of the others. And now ... watching its destruction of our social structure, I am glad I listened to my intuition.

In the end though ... we all have to make the comparison of Social Media to guns ... Social Media doesn't kill people ... *PEOPLE* kill people.

Taking away or heavily regulating the guns will *NOT* fix the problem ... *or* ... make it go away. This is like putting a band-aide on a guy whose just had open heart surgery.

So, how is it that we regulate guns so hard about who uses them and where ... but not Social Media?

It's a sad state of affairs when bureaucrats and politicians and even the media use the deaths of our youth to further some ridiculous agenda ... all the while completely ignoring the real problem by drawing attention to the guns. If you doubt that, then explain why when someone uses an M16-type rifle in a mass shooting, they call for a ban on ALL of these types of "Assault Weapons" ... *but* when a man entered a McDonald's in Washington, D.C. and killed 22 people with a shotgun ... NOT ONE cry was heard to "Ban all shotguns"!

Okay ... let's say we did take away all the "black guns" from the market ... Do you think the online bullying will stop?

Of course it won't.

So ... do you think because we took away all those "evil"-looking guns that the shootings will stop?

Of course they won't.

The age-old adage applies ... *"Guns don't kill people, People kill people."*

Perhaps next time ... the "shooter" will come with a shotgun ... or a crossbow ... or a handgun ... or a kitchen knife even.

The weapon has *nothing* to do with it ... They *will* come.

And when that happens ... then what?

Even if you eventually took away ALL of those weapons ... you STILL have not addressed the problem!

If a man runs his car through a crowd of people in anger (This has happened many, many times), do we ever say *"Let's ban ALL automobiles!"*?

Of course we don't.

That wouldn't make *any* sense ... now would it?

I hope, dear Reader, that you see the ignorance of all this. People are getting angry at an inanimate object that does absolutely nothing until it is picked up and operated by a human! It is the *HUMANS* that we need to fix!

Taking those objects away is not only a waste of time ... it actually prolongs the real problem because all that time, effort and energy was spent doing that instead of fixing the real problem.

Hasn't this bullying's negative and even deadly effects become clearly apparent ... *especially* among our youth?

All of the goings on (suicides, SHOOTING rampages in Schools, etc.) *all* induced by bullying online, have somehow inspired me to coin the phrase "(Anti)Social Media". Feel free to use it and maybe it will open some eyes.

Hasn't this gone on long enough?

I hope the world wakes up.

In The Company of Thieves

I once aligned with a band of gypsy thieves
and we worked so well together.
We stole and we robbed …
and we robbed and we stole …
Perfection … as birds of a feather.

Each and every time they'd wind up in my town
our villainy grew greater and bolder.
I did my best to keep up with them,
as I was quite a bit older.

I don't see them 'round the block these days …
In fact, as of late … I've heard nothing at all.
No "Fuck you" … No letters …
Not even a "Goodbye" …
No emails, nor a text or a call.

And so here we are … in our brave new world
where convenience dictates the theft of once-sacred-kinship.
"Friend" … "Unfriend" … no effort whatsoever …
You simply crack your mouse like a whip.

And oh, what a painful hole it's made …
This hole in my heart that it leaves.
There is seemingly no honor left anymore …
Not even honor among thieves.

Loyalty?

Memories?

Picayune at present … It's all about "I, Me, Mine".
And why feel troubled
by this death of communication …
when all in your world is fine?

What a sad and vacant lot some newer souls seem to be.
Heartfelt closeness, now a tradition-turned-folklore from the past.
Weeds and leaves slowly covering them up …
with no real love ever built there to last.
And *still* … my heart … dictates that I miss them.

This is my generational piece about the sad state of affairs that (Anti)social media has brought upon the youth of today. As I said in the previous notes, I am appalled that the politicians and bureaucrats would rather make gun laws than address this horrible scourge. IMHO, THIS is the REAL root of the problem causing these mindless shootings.

And NOBODY is addressing this!

WHY?

If in the name of commerce, then we have slipped into a very much darker time than even I am imagining right now ...

Their obsession with this mindless, empty lifestyle has made them all but sociopathic. They engage in whisper campaigns and organized, yes ORGANIZED, bullying in order to keep themselves and their "followers" in some sort of twisted and depraved "pecking order" on a scale the likes of which no generation before has EVER witnessed. It has, and continues to, cause the victims of this pack mentality to commit harm to others in backlash and even SUICIDE to be freed from its hateful and tormenting assault.

Their starving search for acknowledgment, recognition, validation and respect has led them to posting "shock"-type behaviors, like showing their "junk", or some ill-gotten loot or another person in a compromising or embarrassing situation ... and even threatening (and now carrying out) SHOOTINGS! All in their screaming request for attention.

BUT ... this need can NEVER be fulfilled by a cold, glass screen. The very thing they are seeking these desperately needed things from IS, in fact, the VERY THING that is, and will continue to, KEEP them from it!

They are losing touch with their own feelings and sadder still, what it means to have a real life and a real friend!

I've YET to see a screen that can reach out and give you a HUG!

Also, this work has NOTHING to do with the Band called Company of Thieves. They are good friends of mine and I speak to Marc, the guitarist all the time. I simply "stole" their moniker (and the very idea of that phrase) and a few minutia's about them, mischievously, to use as a vehicle to tell this tale about how the youth of today don't HAVE friendships, they STEAL them, literally AND figuratively! They "collect" friends online like baseball cards ... and the relationship is about as meaningful.

I LOVE the way it turned out. It was perfect.

If you've never heard of this band, you will. If you don't wish to wait, just Google them or better still, search for a play list or their new EP "Better Together" on You Tube. They are one of my all-time favorite bands and just NOTHING short of AMAZING!

You can (and will) thank me later!

(Yes, yes ... TWO rants in a row. Sorry dear Reader ... but this issue makes my blood boil!)

Et Tu, Brute?

"Et tu, Brute?"

"Et tu, Brute?" is a Latin phrase meaning: "And you, Brutus?". It is notable for its occurrence in William Shakespeare's play "Julius Caesar", where it is spoken by the Roman dictator to his close friend Marcus Junius Brutus at the moment of Caesars assassination. The phrases first known occurrences are said to be in two earlier Elizabethan plays: an early play by Shakespeare and an even earlier play that is now lost.

In modern times, the phrase has become known to signify the sudden or unexpected betrayal by a friend. Caesar utters these words in Act III, Scene I, as he is being stabbed to death and recognizes his friend and protege, Brutus, as one of the assassins.

~Wikipedia

It has to be said, that several of these pieces are me venting or being sad or bitter.

Okay, okay, dear Reader … a *cry baby*, even.

In those cases, I'm being selfish or self-centered. Mea Culpa. But, as they say, "What's done, is done". I guess the surprise (read: shock) of having that happen to me, as well as the selfish realization that that person is now missing from my life, made me write them. I value my friends on the highest level. *But* … I must confess: I too, am guilty of *not* being as a good of a friend as I should be sometimes.

Aren't we all?

Well, I write what comes to me and sometimes it's these … After all, I do write therapeutically as often as not. I am also guilty of "beating a dead horse" and will try to reach out to this person, not wanting to let go.

Now, I'm not talking about break ups from girlfriends, stealing from me or other things in this instance. I'm talking about people that inexplicably just change who they are with or towards me, for whatever reason. People who seem really *close* to me and then just disappear or become indifferent towards me.

Understandably, it will never cease to confound, or hurt, me. The pain of realizing that a friendship was predicated on convenience or whatever, is really hurtful, especially when it wasn't predicated by that to *you* … but it happens.

It just is what it is.

I also have to admit that I too, have done this to others for my own, albeit, non-nefarious reasons. Perhaps we were just never around one another anymore or whatever. Still … I would talk to them any time, as to me, friendships are forever, no matter the distance. But still, when it happens to me, I have to ask … is this my Karma?

Oh … I would bet money on it.

~Jeff

Forgotten ... But Not Gone

I felt blessed to have witnessed your star being born ...
adoration filling my gaze.
The fading light in my tired, old eyes,
was re-lit by its rays.

I helped you climb into the heavens
so that you could take your place in the sky.
Your words, old soul and innocent smile,
helped my weary wings to fly.

I was certain from that moment I first looked in your eyes,
that I had known you through all of time.
Crossing paths again and again ...
your lives, entwined in mine.

Weeks sharing stories ...
Hours sharing laughs ...
and some days, dark secrets were told.
Although we barely just had met,
our connection felt comfortably old.

We talked on for months of home and of pain ...
and of dreams that we wished to see.
No other friendship in this whole life,
had ever meant so much to me.

As I watched you ascend into the sky,
the thought never crossed my mind ...
that when you alit on your lofty perch,
you would leave me so far behind.

Had I imagined our guild?

Was I befriended ... *or fooled*?

Tell me, how can this be?

To this very day, I can *still* see those eyes ...
but *you* ...
have forgotten *me*.

I wonder ... who are you now?

CLXXXIX

Sometimes When You Steal

Sometimes when you steal,
You can end up ahead . . .

But why take the bonus from one opportunity
And trade it,
For the lifetime of opportunities you could have had,
With the person you stole from?

Could it possibly be worth it?

Besides . . .
Sometimes when you steal,
You can end up *dead* . . .

When I lived in my beautiful cottage by the river, the old house across the street had been converted into a "flophouse", much like what unscrupulous landlords do in the 5 boroughs of NYC. They take a studio and make it a 3 bedroom ... they take a two bedroom and make it a 5 and ... well, you get the picture. The owner of this home had done the same.

SO, being low rent for being crammed into such a small space with others, it attracted ne'er-do-well's and transients ... at best. One morning I awoke to sirens and such invading my normally quiet and peaceful, dead end street. Apparently, a guy had been stabbed to death in the flop house ...

A MURDER in my quaint little fishing village?

NO!

But, it was all confirmed by one of the local Police Officers there that was also a pal of mine. He told me that one of the "flops" was actually renting the couch and that another 'tenant' had placed a beer in the fridge for his early morning shakes.

When he awoke and found it missing, he saw an empty one of the same brand beside the guy on the couch. Infuriated that the guy took his beer, he repeatedly plunged a 10-inch kitchen knife into the guy in his sleep ... The poor soul never woke up.

What was really sad, was that it all came out somehow that it was NOT his beer and that the stabber's beer had been drunk by the stabber's own female "house guest" while he was asleep. I'm guessing her shakes came earlier than his? Somehow, I'm reminded here of the W.C. Fields line: "*Ah, the evils of strong drink!*"

Also during that time in my life, I had helped two "friends" that were really struggling ... who, in turn, had then stolen from me ... one opportunistically (Not a story even worth telling, but a bitter disappointment nonetheless) and the other refusing to pay me back after I had bought him a used car to help get him back on his feet. He got a great job paying exceptional money and just ignored me afterwards.

I had kept breakfast food, coffee, drinks, P, B & J and cold cuts in the kitchen for him while he crashed on my couch. I even took him out to the pub when I had the extra loot. I was doing well ... he had fallen on hard times. I loved helping him, he was my friend. At least I had always thought he was.

He disappeared the day he was to get his first paycheck. I didn't see him again until someone told me where he had rented an apartment. I dropped by to see him and he wouldn't take his eyes off the TV. The rest of the story tells itself. Those frustrating "lessons" and the poor guy on the couch across the street became this piece in my often-hard-to-understand mind. I know that he didn't actually steal the beer, but the parable, as-it-were, remains.

On The Renouncement of a Sunflower

I came to life in a field,
happy to be me …
in the light that shares my namesake.

Glowing like a smile,
for all to see …
and for any soul to take.

I arrived, en masse …
in a painted tin cart,
sent with hopes of brightening a room.

A gift of love,
with a note from the heart …
encouraging your dreams to resume.

Then you placed me in your kitchen …
your nature still veiled …
from the outstretched arms of a friend.

For my meaning meant nothing …
a ship long sailed …
something you'd broken, refusing to mend.

I withered, dying there,
having given it my all …
the very best that I could.

Then tossed in the bin,
with our communion-turned-wall …
still … hoping I had done something good.

Unable to fathom …
Too guarded to call …
Sad … that I never would.

As you closed that lid, you closed your eyes,
making sure that you'd not have to see …
that the spirit of that Sunflower …
in all of those Sunflowers … lying there … was me.

Clouds

I guess that I misunderstood you.
A brain does this ... now and again.
My heart heard you say that you loved me
and it loved having you here now and then.

But sometimes things are spoken out of context
or simply perceived in a shroud.
A brain clouded by misconception.
A heart seeing shapes in the clouds.

Aside from my ten-word piece, "Clouds" is the shortest poem I've written to date. I'll not go into what inspired it. Sorry, there's just no need on my part, other than to say it is about misunderstanding the intentions of a friend, as-it-were. After some rearranging, as I finished the last line, I looked up and read it through, then saved it, as is. It expressed just what I was trying to say and that was that.

May 20th, 1999 (The Poem)

I had my heart broken today for the last time …
I was snooping … Mea Culpa.
I can't help it … It seems that every time I do, I find what I'm looking for ...
I loved her … but she doesn't understand … if she does, then she hates me.
I can't believe what I found today …
I feel like half of my conscience wants to show me the truth that I've known for almost a year.
I also feel the other half wants to pretend that everything is normal and OK.
Because I, like everyone else, need to love and be loved.
I never mistreated her … at least that's what she says.
I never deserved the lies and deceit … at least that's what she says.
I never understood, no matter how hard I tried.
I communicated, I negotiated, I pleaded, I even quit the relationship … but she always came back.
I took her back each time … the reasons were many:
I felt that she understood my frustration and that she felt bad.
I felt that maybe she could sense the loss of my love and actually missed it.
I felt that she finally understood that my patience and understanding of her painful, unexplained crimes was really my trying to understand her issues and still stand beside her.
I even felt that maybe she could understand that my being there through all of this was because I loved her.
I took her back willingly each time, thinking that at last we were going to once again share the love I tried so hard to show her.
I remember feeling, many times that it was time to move on, but she always lured me back.
I loved her more than any woman I had ever been with.
I worked harder on this relationship than any other in my life.
I read the poem for the first time the day she gave it to me.
I looked at the title … "Jeff Gaines"
I was so flattered … I had tears in my eyes.
I read the words and the tears leapt to my cheeks.
I caressed the golden frame she had mounted it in.
I looked into her eyes … flattered that she could write such a beautiful thing … about ME!
I can't say that any one had EVER done such a thing.
I hung it on the wall in my living room at my cottage by the river for all the

world to see.

I wanted them to see it; it was the most beautiful poem I had ever read. How could this be about me?

I would read it and my insides would get all warm and fuzzy.

I couldn't hide the joy on my face as I read the words … over and over again.

I could never put into words what that poem meant to me.

I could never put into words what the girl who'd wrote it had meant to me.

I could definitely never put into words how it made me feel to think that I had inspired those words …

I told you earlier … Mea Culpa. Mea máxima culpa …

I was snooping …

I found that poem in a spiral notebook … from her days in high school.

I found that she had written it about, and for, someone else.

I found that it made me feel like our whole relationship was a lie.

I couldn't, for the life of me, figure out why she had been with me, or what she wanted from me.

I looked back through the time we spent together and I remembered all the lies and games I had to deal with, never giving up, because I believed in this relationship … and her.

I always tried to make her feel confident in my feelings for her.

I felt like she always tried to make me doubt.

I found that as I read the words in her own handwriting, it finished what was left of my heart and it finished what love I had left for her.

I didn't think it was possible.

I couldn't believe that the biggest, most painful lie she'd ever told me … was hanging on my wall.

I envied *him*.

In all honesty, I wasn't snooping. It just worked easier in the composition to not explain that. But I will here. I was sitting at the computer desk in our apartment. On my left was a 3 foot wide, 3-shelf, book case. It was filled with ring-binder notebooks of hers. Probably more than 100! She'd told me they were her "Notes from school" and I never gave them another thought. I had never touched one in over 4 years.

But that day, I had found something online that I wanted to write down. The printer tray was empty, so I looked around for a scrap of paper and figured I might find a blank sheet in one of these notebooks. I randomly grabbed one that had a larger ring in its spine, because it was easier to grab. I put it on my lap and opened it to a random page ... RIGHT to that poem.

Once again, the universe showing me things I am in desperate need of seeing. It was one of the sadder moments in my life, I must say. I opened MS Word and wrote the date at the top. Then I cut loose with whatever came out. The format of every line beginning with "I" just happened ... I left it, as is, and that was that.

"Wow"

I made friends with a shooting star one fine morning …
at least I thought that I did.
It touched me like a real, heartfelt emotion … and not just some winning bid.

From the moment I found her, 'til that last parting shot …
in between, all the here's and now's …
There is just one word to describe it all … and that would simply be *"Wow"*.

Unbounded … by all this new stardom …
it seemingly went straight to her head.
Confounded … I watched her drifting away from me …
swearing it's nothing that I've done or said.

The more new fans and friends that she gathered …
the less of her endearment I'd see.
Her eyes quit lighting up, as they had always done, when she'd come racing up
just to hug me.

I hung in there though … steadfast and true … I never, *ever* wavered.
But, it seemed, no matter what I did … I was slowly, but surely, less favored.

I did all that I could to help her star climb …
Oh, but with that, up came her wall.
I watched her latest mask become someone else …
a persona I didn't care for at all.

Finally one day, she disappeared me for a year,
retreating, deep inside her shell …
This was my perplexing lot.

Ever true … and the fiercest of friends, I just had to give it one last shot.

A shallow excuse … then a pair of lies …
and a reprise back to the cold, painful silence …

After all the times shared and things done and said …
That … was all that I got.

She had dismissed my loyalty, and all of my love …
Though hurt, I'd been patient to a fault.
It just goes to show you that no matter how hard you try …
you can't teach a turtle to waltz.

And now it's all finished … a sad, lonely fruition …
confident … I have done all that I can.
Totally dumbfounded at this juxtaposition …
Devoted … uncommon friend … Demoted … to some common fan.

Sadly, I could *never, ever* be one of those …
nor waste my time annoying some poor turtle.
Sadder still … I never got to tell the *real* her "Goodbye";
She'd meant the world to me.

I once had a really close friend ... I really want to believe this ... BUT ... No matter how close I thought that I was ... I would soon learn I was wrong. and eventually, after years of what I thought was closeness, she just "vanished" from me (or did she "vanish" me from her?), leaving me no way to contact her.

I pondered the reasons to the point of insanity ... until a mutual friend helped me realize that it just was what it was and there was nothing to do or say except to write a therapeutic piece like this (a few, actually) and move on.

I was also led to find this writing from poet Trent Shelton ... It truly began my healing process with an enlightened understanding:

"You can't control someone's loyalty. Being loyal is a decision they have to make. No matter how good you are to them, doesn't mean they'll treat you the same. No matter how much they mean to you, doesn't mean they'll value you the same. You just have to understand the people you love the most, can sometimes turn out to be the people you can trust the least. But never let that turn you into a person you're not. Keep LOVE in your heart."
~Trent Shelton

As sad as the inspiration for this piece is, I am really proud of it. In particularly, the wordsmithing. I intentionally tried to make the wording go all over the place. I wanted it to almost look random, with each verse being structured differently than the last. I also went a bit loopy with the syllables. One of the verses actually having 27! I didn't want it to even appear like a poem ... and yet, when you read it, it all flows seamlessly.

The reason for all this was to relay what it was like dealing with the muse ... while all seemed to flow normally, she never really let you get her completely into focus. No matter how clear it all seemed ... it never actually was.

To call her aloof, would be the understatement of the century. But her talent is ... she doesn't *seem* aloof whatsoever. She makes you feel close. You *feel* like you have her arm around you ... but you are actually at its length. One of the most amazing defense mechanisms I've ever encountered.

I don't have any animosity for her whatsoever. I'm all but sure that she has none for me either and I would trust her with my life, if it came to that. There may be a little bitterness reflected in the piece, but I was still stinging when I wrote it, so, I guess I'm guilty of that ... and I can't take it back.

People change, it is a natural thing with growth, self discovery, even changes in their lifestyle or surroundings. She will always mean the world to me for my own reasons and she has every right to have, or not have, me in her life. I just wish I understood a little better ... and that it didn't hurt so damn much.

Caprice

I once knew a girl
and she lived in your eyes …
She could see green, greener grass and blue, bluer skies.

I once knew girl
and my soul adored her so …
But tell me now where, just where did she go?

I once knew a girl
and her voice, so proud …
All at once like thunder and soft, softest cloud.

I once knew a girl
and her light, it shined like the sun …
She reveled in challenge and she took every one.

I once knew a girl
and my belief in her was beyond …
But tell me now where, well where has she gone?

I once knew a girl
and her brio, it was just so extreme …
Her dances were made of joyous joy and her smiles …
of pure, purist dreams.

I once knew a girl
and her laughter, it could easily stop a war …
Her conversations so engaging and her appreciation galore.

I once knew a girl
and her heart so brave, it was always showing through …
But somehow, I can't see it now and that's why I'm asking you.

You see, I miss that girl
that once lived in your eyes.
So please, I just need to know …
That girl …
was so very precious to me …
Tell me now …
Where, where did she go?

It is so sad to see someone change and then have to ponder whether this was them becoming someone else … or if they were somehow fooling you all along and that now, you are seeing the real them for the first time.

---

ca·price
kəˈprēs
noun
noun: caprice; plural noun: caprices

1.
a sudden and unaccountable change of mood or behavior.
"Her caprices had made his life impossible"
synonyms: whim, whimsy, vagary, fancy, fad, quirk, eccentricity, foible More

2.
MUSIC
another term for capriccio.

---

ca·pric·ci·o
kəˈprēCHēˌō
noun
noun: capriccio; plural noun: capriccios

1.
a lively piece of music, typically one that is short and free in form.
synonyms: whim, whimsy, vagary, fancy, fad, quirk, eccentricity, foible
2.
a painting or other work of art representing a fantasy or a mixture of real and imaginary features.

Bridges Over Troubled Waters

"All your dreams are on their way
See how they shine
Oh, if you need a friend
I'm sailing right behind
Like a bridge over troubled water
I will ease your mind"

~Paul Simon

Yes ... I've put a subsections inside of a section ... Yes ... I've put short stories inside of the poetry section ...

Surely, you aren't surprised ...

I don't *have* a box ... Remember?

Since they are about this section's "Et Tu, Brute" subject, I felt they needed to be here.

There are no notes at the ends of these two writings. Both are very personal and I just don't think that writing beyond what I've written will help me ... *or* you. I also don't wish to live within them any further than I already have. They both just are what they are. Glean from my experiences what you will, dear Reader. I don't just write these for me ... I write them for you too.

I will say this ...

"The Listening Bridge" was written as a parable, obviously, and I *sent it* to the person who is portrayed by the speeder. It actually made him see things through my eyes and it rebuilt our bridge.

We remain friends to this day and probably will for life. I'm still uncertain where I stand with the other friend.

And *yes* ... I *did* use a bridge as a metaphor in two *different* stories ...

So sue me ...

The Bridge to Joel Madison

I lost a friend today …

At least I think I did … It sure *feels* like I did …

Maybe … I just think too much … At this moment, I don't know *what* to think … it's just that there was such a splash in my ocean today … a soul-soaker …

Joel is one of the few people in my world that I feel doesn't want anything from me. Some one who I really enjoy hanging around with. We share a great many interests … *deeply important* interests …

Flying for instance … We both have the deepest passion for flying airplanes. There are few bugs like it in the world. Once you've been bitten … there is no escape. It is very hard to love anything like you would love flying.

It's so … *well rounded* … this passion … its many facets making a jewel like no other …

Firstly, to be … *up there* …

Looking out over the *rest* of the world … is a serenity only a pilot can understand.

Secondly, to be in control of your motion *while* you are up there … can give you that elusive feeling that most of us philosophically ponder as we watch a bird's flight in wonderment.

And last but not least … With love … any and all loves … there must be respect. So if you truly love flying, you most assuredly respect it. If you don't … it can *kill* you.

It's kind of a strange lesson on real love … Flying I mean … It must be accompanied by respect.

I guess you could compare it to the sea … I also have a deep passion for the sea. I share this with many, many people. Those who love the sea as much as I love flying. I promise that in this love, just as with flying, there is a deep respect.

Again, if there isn't … it can kill you.

But Joel and I *love* flying …

We also share another deeply important interest … Reese's Peanut Butter Cups … *Frozen* Reese's Peanut Butter Cups to be more precise. We always have them in our freezer. When I'm at his house, he throws me a few. When he's at mine, I toss him a couple. We bring them to each other's house and "keep the stock up". There's other stuff too … but you get the picture.

 I'm getting ahead of my self though. First, you must know that I met Joel in the seventh grade … I've known him for over 27 years … you do the math … we're getting older. I've known his wife for over 20 years and knew each of them before they knew each other …

Here is where the story begins with twist … I ran into his wife at a pub about a year and a half ago and before I knew it, I was "meeting her husband" and low and behold I knew him too! That happens a lot around here … I mean me knowing people. I've lived here over 30 years.

When I got here, there were dairy and chicken farms and such. There aren't any of those within fifty miles of here now. I've grown up with the community. I know *a lot* of people. We got to talking, Joel and I … then eventually hanging out … at least when he wasn't working.

I've never seen any one who could "Go" like he can. He is in motion from the time he gets out of bed until the time he climbs back in it … When I say motion … I mean *MOTION!* If he isn't literally at work doing some project, he's hot on the heels of one somewhere around his house.

He and his family helped me move into this old house I'm buying. He had his paid employee, Wendell, come and help me do stuff around here to get the ol' place ready for me to move in. His wife and kids even helped move furniture or clean or paint.

I was so flattered that they'd help me like this … I was amazed at how strong the bridge between he and I had been … Without seeing him for years, we were buddies just like we'd been years ago. I wondered if it was a lingering emotion carried over from our youth … or did he, like me, just believe in being real.

I thought it was a little of both. Let's face it, as you grow older, those types of friendships grow fewer and farther between. Every one wants something out of you or has some motive for befriending you. Of course, the more successful you are, the more of these "non-real" types you attract.

Your older, more "real" friends seem to head off in their own directions and rarely do you get to keep an "old" friend in your life for any length of time. I think we both thought it odd that we'd known each other for so long and yet not seen each other around this little town for years! And besides all that ... share a passion for flying, as well.

This is where our parallel lives ended though. You see, he'd gotten his GED and left school in eighth grade. He hated school and wanted to get right to work! Like I said ... always in motion. I loved school and stayed to graduate. By the time I was out of school and started working as a heavy equipment operator, building roads, he was working at a restaurant his uncle owned and driving a 'Vette! After that, he went into construction. He's done very well for himself that Joel.

He has provided for himself and his family with great success. He has a nice house and he and his wife have four kids. They have many nice things ... like four-wheel ATV's ... A nice motor coach for the whole family to go camping in ... and an airplane.

His construction experience helped him get a contractor's license, a busy industry here in west central Florida ... as is keeping up with four kids and a wife ... a pool ... two cats, a dog, several fish, two turtles and six ATV's, a golf cart, a motorcycle, a motor coach, an airplane *and* an airport. Did I mention that they live on a runway? His subdivision has it's own airport and most of the people who live there have their own airplanes.

Leave it to Joel ... He's in charge of maintaining the airport. He changes bulbs on the runway, orders fuel, makes purchases and such, all while juggling the rest of his life. No problem for him though ... Always in motion. He is truly amazing.

I went another route entirely ... chasing dreams and pots of gold, changing careers whenever the wind blew. I've never really had anything. I've always rented. I've even lived in my car when times were tough. I've never accumulated anything but experiences. To have the things he has ... *especially* a family ... has always been my most elusive dream ... let alone to have an airplane and live *on* a runway!

I have no regrets though and neither does he ...

But on more than one occasion we've each laughingly expressed a jealousy for each other's lives ...

Me, filled with a longing for security ...

He, filled with a longing to be a leaf on the wind ...

Ah ... sweet irony ... I think we are both just a little tired ...

Hindsight is always 20/20 when you're looking at the green, green grass ... on the other side of the fence.

For his help, I tried many a time to show my appreciation ... but no matter what I did, I felt like I was annoying him more than anything. Furthermore, they always made me feel so welcome in their home, calling me over all the time and whatnot. I loved it. It gave me a feeling of belonging to a family that I had been missing for *far* too many years.

They made me feel so comfortable. I loved his children like they were my own. I tried to help him whenever I could ... but more often than not, it would seem, I caused more harm than good. I settled for just hanging out and trying to let them know if they needed anything, to just ask. I sometimes opted to stay out of his way when he was busy with something and just sit up in the office and play on the computer.

After a while, I noticed a change in the kid's demeanor towards me. They began to talk to and treat me with great disrespect. One day the older son, angry because I wouldn't let him bully his younger brother off of the computer, told me that he " ... couldn't understand why my parents let you come over at all."

When I asked what he meant by that, he replied that they thought I was a jerk. I was dumbfounded. I didn't know if this bordering-on-genius-IQ child was using the sharp sword of a child's tongue to lash out at me, or if this was the black and white world of youth. But later my suspicious fears began to be confirmed.

One by one, the kids each began to show me not only disrespect, but also an outright pleasure in aggravating me by hiding my things, vandalizing my car or just plain saying mean, spiteful things. When I told their parents what had happened, I was amazed that there was very little … if any … reprehension.

I began to theorize that the children had heard their parents speaking badly of me in my absence and so they felt that they had "license" to disrespect me.

And why not?

If their parents thought so little of me … why should they show me any respect?

Especially when I was trying to stop them from fighting with one another or bullying each other. They felt they didn't have to listen to me because their parents didn't hold a very high opinion of me.

When you are their age, your behaviors are learned … by example. I had never seen this disrespectful demeanor being displayed to any of the other "adults" in their world. I didn't want to believe my theory … I wanted to be part of this family and Joel's friendship meant the world to me.

I started to not hang out at the house so much. I thought that maybe it would be better. Maybe I was getting on their nerves. I would tell them to call me … but the calls would never come. When they did, they would say things like " … *you* were supposed to call *us*." Or " … How come you ain't been coming over to hang out lately?"

More confusion … I didn't want to confront them with what I was thinking.

What if I was wrong?

What if it was just the kids being kids … or me, like I said before, "thinking too much"?

So I slowly started coming back over, but my friendship with the kids wasn't the same. I kept my guard up and didn't interact with them as much. It hurt like hell …

One week, Wendell had to go out west. His mom was very sick. I went to work with Joel in his place to try and help him meet a deadline on a very important client's new home. It was summer and Joel brought along his younger son. I'd always gotten along great with him … protecting him from his older brother's bullying. But the first day out on the job site … I asked him to run and grab a can of PVC glue.

He not only smarted off to me … When I told him not to talk to me like I was an idiot … He informed me: "You *are* and idiot!"

I couldn't believe he was speaking to me like that. But that was nothing compared to the disbelief that I was smacked with when I told Joel what the boy had said to me and Joel said little if anything to him about it. When I was a child, if I spoke with disrespect to an elder I was punished post haste.

For the rest of the day, I wondered if there would have been more said if the boy had spouted off to another of Joel's adult friends … The older sons words from before floated around under my bridge all the way home that day …

"If they don't want me around … " I thought. " … then why call or invite me … or ask me why I wasn't coming over as much?" More-so … "Why help me out so much?" The confusion blended into a cocktail with my fears and my pain that made me ill.

I hung out less and less … I didn't know what else to do. This time, they called less and less.

My theory was proving to be more and more correct all the time.

But did he … *they* … really hate me or think so little of me that they had no respect for me at all?

After all … love, *true* love … comes with respect.

Remember?

I never had a bad word to say about any of them … especially Joel. He was one of the best friends I had! How could it be that right in front of me … he was teaching his kids that he had no respect for me?

I didn't know what to think.

I've said before that we are all islands.

To go along with that, I'd like to add that between us we have bridges.

Some are weak …

Some are strong …

Some are short …

Some are long …

We build them …

We propose them …

And sometimes … we *burn* them …

In the business world, they call it "networking" … But, no matter what its name, the stronger the bridge we build with someone, the more weight that can be carried across it.

These weights can be burdens or blessings … it's what the bridge's are for. It's what helps to keep us friends and allows us to do for one another … to help carry each others weight … to share each others blessings. The bridge's ability to hold weight is a direct measure of the strength of a friendship and the mutual respect that comes with it.

I was fascinated that our bridge had remained through all those years … Or did it?

Today I was at the house and had a few final bricks of evidence dropped on my head.

Again, by the kids …

A few days before, I had sat up for hours in the office on the phone trying to get their new cable internet connection straight. Half of the time on hold, the other half talking to a technician. After that, the younger son asked me to put some games on his desktop. The older one, always the bully, then went behind me, deleting them. In his blind cruelty, he deleted the game's ability to be played by any one.

When I called him on it, he spitefully informed me that he had heard his dad telling some friends, who were visiting for the weekend, that he " … Hate's it when Jeff comes over because he's always on the computer and so he can't get on it to get his own work done."

I could tell not only by the look on his face that he was telling the truth, but by the fact that when I met these people, that they never really bonded with me. Hardly looking me in the eye, short in conversation, cold body language etc. But, more than anything else I'd noticed, was this overwhelming feeling that they knew something that I didn't.

I can't explain it, but I get "Vibes" (for lack of a better term) from people. Well now it was all explained. These people felt no respect for me because they felt no respect for me from Joel … *Just* like the kids. After this realization, I left and went home with a broken heart. My usually overactive mind was going a million miles an hour …

What had I done?

What had I said?

What could have possibly transpired to make him *secretly* dislike me so much?

Stranger still … Why do so much for some one you seemingly cared so little for?

He had done so much for me …

I had nothing to offer him in return but my friendship … My respect.

It made no sense to me at all …

But the writing was on the wall … as clear as day.

A few hours later, his older daughter called me, having a dilemma on the computer while trying to get on the net to do a book report. I drove back out there to help her and while I was there, the older boy asked me to help him do something on the net … I informed him that since he didn't appreciate my helping him any other time, I didn't see any reason why I should help him now.

He stated that it wasn't him who didn't appreciate what I did on the machine.

He topped that off by informing me that, at the dinner table earlier that night, the younger brother (The one who I had helped by putting games on his desktop) had made the statement: "Why doesn't scumbag Jeff get his own computer, instead of using ours?"

I *had* my own computer … I was always over *there* helping *them* with *theirs.*

The older daughter wouldn't even look away from the computer … She wouldn't look at me. It confirmed that she knew that what he was saying was true. She *knew* it was said.

I just shook my head.

The bully didn't even realize that it wasn't *only* his brother that he was telling on.

She knew *that* too. *That's* why she wouldn't look up at me.

How could a ten-year-old kid feel *so* comfortable calling an adult friend of his parents "Scumbag" … right in *front* of them?

It just all made *too* much sense …

More sense than I cared to deal with …

And with those few simple words …

From the mouths of a few small boys …

I felt a bridge crumble … into the ocean.

A bridge that had meant so much to me …

A bridge that I so desperately wanted to stay intact …

Soaking my soul with painful, bone chilling waves …

It was a very large splash indeed …

The Listening Bridge

There once were two lifelong pals and one day, one of them built a bridge, so that he and his friend wouldn't have to chat across a wide, deep river. It wasn't a fancy bridge. but it was sturdy and did the job well. Soon after building it, he noticed his pal racing over top of it, shaking it to its very foundation. When he asked his pal why he had done that, he replied: "Oh, I didn't know that I should go slower; sorry". The builder smiled and said "No, problem. I just don't want the bridge to break down as you are my best friend and I like your company".

But the next day, he watched his pal speeding over the fragile bridge again. Confounded, he asked him: "Why?" … and the pal responded nonchalantly: "Oh, my throttle stuck". The builder asked him to fix his throttle so as to keep from speeding over the bridge … patiently, but urgently repeating how important it was to him. His pal assured him that he would.

The very next day, the builder looked out the window only to see his pal, again, speeding over the bridge. Now, truly upset, he calmly, but sternly, asked his friend why he was repeatedly speeding over the bridge after he had asked him not to and, more frustratingly, even after he had explained to him why it was so important to him that he not speed over the bridge. The friend looked at him and became very defensive saying:

"You are really over reacting here! I have gone over the bridge fast with no issues so far. So, it can not be such a big deal!"
The builder said: "I have explained to you that it is a very big issue to me and that the bridge is weakening and will not repeatedly take this abuse, so I fear it will collapse."

The pal replied, "Well, I was upset with my job and I took it out on my car. So yes, I was speeding. Sorry. But, it's not really my fault."

The builder felt there was nothing to say to such a explanation and let it go … hoping that it would eventually stop.

But, sure enough, the next day, he looked out to see him speeding over the bridge yet again … He watched the fragile bridge shake and bow under the stress. He shook his head in anger and frustration and asked his pal once again … "Why?"

This time, the friend responded in an loud angry voice, screaming at the builder … **"WHY IS THIS SUCH A BIG DEAL TO YOU, MAN?"**

"I DONT THINK IT'S SUCH A BIG DEAL AND BESIDES, I WAS FRUSTRATED THAT MY KIDS KEEP PESTERING ME FOR MONEY; SO I WAS UPSET AND DRIVING FAST … " His tone was bitter and menacing … he seemed absolutely annoyed … **"BUT I'M NOT DOING IT ON PURPOSE. SO, IT'S NOT MY FAULT! MY GOD MAN, JUST DEAL WITH IT!"**

The builder stepped back, aghast in frustration … feeling bad for his friends problems and hoping it would all soon pass for him … and their friendship … *and* the bridge.

But … the very next day, he couldn't believe his eyes …. his pal was *again* speeding over the bridge. He confronted him, and this time, it was HE who was angrily shouting and asking why he continued to speed over the bridge, no matter how many times he asked him not to.

The pal looked at him and aggressively shouted back that the builder was "seriously messed up" for thinking that his speed was excessive and that he "shouldn't make such a big deal out of it" because he "wasn't doing anything on purpose". The builders old pal then finished with: "So, if you feel I'm speeding too often over *your* bridge and it's bothering you so much, then maybe you need to tear it down!"

He got in his car and sped back over the bridge, as the builder stood there … silent … sadly bewildered. He looked and listened to the rushing river and pondered aloud …

"I thought … it was our bridge."

The next day, the old pal came to a screeching halt and climbed out of his car to look at the open space where the bridge once stood … his lifelong friend had taken it down.

He looked across the river at his pal and yelled simply "Why?"

The builder looked back across the river and humbly … *Honestly* … responded.

"Because, you are my dear friend … and that is what you told me I needed to do."

Reality Check

"People will always make time for those
that they truly want to make time for;
As people intrinsically fulfill their own wishes
and desires each and every day ...
Be it with food, drink *or* friends.

Never, ever believe anyone who says they have just been too busy.
The honest fact of the matter is that
if they truly wished to speak to you ...
or involve you in their lives for that matter ...
they would find the time ... or a way ... to do just that.
People get what they want ... mostly.

However ... there is something here that
we must all keep in mind ...
It is their *right* as a being to *not* have us in their lives.
It isn't our choice ... It is theirs.

That being said, you have no right ... whatsoever ...
To feel angry about their decision.
No matter how much it hurts ... it is what it is ...
You can only accept and respect it."

~Jeff Gaines

"We all lose friends.. we lose them in death, to distance, and over time. But even though they may be lost, hope is not. The key is to keep them in your heart, and when the time is right, you can pick up the friendship right where you left off. Even the lost find their way home, when you leave the light on."

~Amy Marie Walz

All of the pieces in this "Et Tu, Brute" section deal with feeling betrayed or having someone change or turn on you (me). Frustrating, even painful, to be sure. But ... things happen. People change and quite often circumstances in their lives can make them do inexplicable things. These can confound you, hurt you or even make you angry. Admittedly ... I have been on both sides of this coin.

If it has effected me that much, as I've told you, I quite often write "therapeutic" pieces, as I call them. It lets me vent and it helps me come to terms with the issue. But, in my view, if a person hasn't deliberately hurt me or stolen from me, or whatever ... they simply "changed" and drifted from my life ... then I don't hold it against them. No matter how hurt or angry I may seem in my poems or writings, you must keep in mind that this is me venting and coming to terms with what has happened, like I said.

To show you what I mean, and to prove that I truly don't hold a grudge about it, I placed this last piece, a poem titled "The Rope" here, in "Et Tu, Brute" instead of "On Being Me", because it is how I feel about handling these types of things when friends "need" to change. It is, in its entirety, the exact way that I presented it on Hello Poetry.

I do believe that if that person does decide to take up the friendship again, then it is always worth it to try. Having a friend is *always* better than not having a friend ... Wouldn't you agree?

Honestly, I wrote this poem with a specific person being the muse, but it does apply to all. I hope its meaning resonates with you, dear Reader, on some level.

~Jeff

The Rope

We weaved this rope from tears ...
of joy and of pain.
On each other ... we would depend.

Our hands working
in unison ... weaving
over and under ...
again and again and again.

Our rope
built with love and dedication ...
can withstand any strain.

Yet, this rope that we've made
is warm and supple to the hands ...
not cold and hard like a chain.

It has held us together ...
It has lifted us up ...
even lowered us gently to the ground.

Built to chase dreams, this rope of ours ...
none greater could ever be found.

Our rope is ever our most useful tool ...
Soft but strong and sound.

Its uses seemingly endless ... and yet,
never ever was it used to bound.

Our rope ... Our bond ...
Us against the world ... and I'll always wish it to be so.

I never imagined ... not even for a moment ...
that either of us ...
could ever, ever let go.

I will linger here ... until time disappears ...
diligently holding my end.
If you have become lost somehow, I want you to know ...
the rope ... our rope ...
awaits you right here, my friend.

If you truly believe in a person … then for goodness sake … no matter WHAT they do … NEVER … EVER give up on them. I'll never tell you what to do or how to live your life. Only you, in the end, can decide what transgressions you can accept and forgive … or if the persons friendship is worth the effort.

People have a millions reasons why they do things. Sometimes it is valid and sometimes it isn't. But if they discover that they made a mistake … and you aren't there to help pull it back together … then you BOTH lose out.

Yes it is frustrating.

Yes, it is painful.

But as I said …

If you believe in them and your friendship … DO NOT GIVE UP ON THEM!

On Being Me

"Suffering has been stronger than all other teaching, and has taught me to understand what your heart used to be. I have been bent and broken, but ... I hope ... into a better shape."

~Charles Dickens

Searcher

I'm looking for something ...

and I don't ever know if I'll know what it is.

Maybe I'm just supposed to see all the things you can search for,
and yet,
never really *have* anything.

Just *see* everything.

I can accept that ...

I've had an *outrageous* life so far.

Like "For Ethereal ...", This is an actual excerpt from an online chat that I was having with an old High School classmate. After I looked up and read what I had just written to her in the little window, I was struck by it so hard, that I cut and pasted it right into MSWord and made it into one of my "pieces". We had been chatting about where we had been and how our lives were going at that moment.

She had just settled into her new marriage, her new home and her new pregnancy. She had asked me if I thought I ever wanted, or longed for, "the family life" or just to settle down.

I never did find that life. After learning of my condition all these years later, I don't see myself ever having a "family life", as that wouldn't be fair to my "family". A father and husband needs to be around. Starting a family or even a serious relationship while knowing they would have to watch you pass away is just plain wrong.

Still, like the piece says, I am content with just seeing "everything".

I really expounded on this concept in "Restless".

I wrote both long before I learned that I was sick. So, I guess accepting my new "situation" came a bit easier, in its own way ... as if the Universe knew what it was doing all along.

If I Could Just Fly

I wish I could fly above mountains so high,
soaring with laughter,
caressing the sky.

I'd fly when in boredom,
in sorrow
or pain.
I'd fly in the moonlight.
I'd fly in the rain.

I wish I could fly
through clouds so white ...
warm in the sunshine
and cool at night.

I'd fly over houses
and people
and trees.
I'd fly all directions
with Falcons and Bees.

I wish I could fly over buildings so tall,
with no need to catch me
if I should fall.

I'd fly over pastures
and canyons
and streams.
I'd fly through some hurricanes,
I'd fly through some dreams.

I wish I could fly, just up and take flight.
I wish I could soar with all of my might.

I'd fly when I'm lonesome,
tearful
or mad.
It would make me happy,
cheerful
and glad.

CCXXIX

If I could just fly …
Lord knows I've tried.
I'd never stop flying,
'til the day that I died.

Haven't we *all* had this dream at some time or another?

Put The Needle On The Record!

There are no words
that can describe
how music makes me feel.

It's always been there
touching something
deep inside that's real.

From watching my Mom
bopping to Motown
vacuuming our wooden floor.

To fishing through a thousand dance singles
when I was a DJ
hanging at the record store.

Always a banging stereo
in all of my cars.
Loud as hell down at the beach.

There is just this spot
deep in my soul
that music seems to reach.

I once collected
over twenty-thousand records.
But have since culled that herd.

Now I've maybe a thousand CD's.
On my 'puter, a bazillion songs.
I guess I'm a digital nerd.

From fist pumps
to goosebumps
it brings all these compulsive things.

It makes us laugh

It makes us cry
and to our heart it clings.

If you ever
took my music away
it wouldn't be just a crime.

You may as well
put me outta my misery
as I'd simply lose my mind.

I love it all
Classical, Pop, Rock, Techno.
Even Country and Blue Grass.

But when it comes to Gangster Rap
and most newer Hip Hop
I'll have to take a pass.

It's not just about the often-poser "thugs"
that make it
spreading hate and acting all corrupt.

It just sounds to me
all lyrically the same
and so creatively bankrupt.

After Buffalo Stance
it started rolling down hill
and is just running out of gas.

All this chest beating
about guns and ho's
it simply has no class.

Such a magnificent notion
this music phenomenon
that we all love.

I'd bet you would stand and fight
to keep it in your life

if push should come to shove.

Like poetry
or any other art
it lets us bare our souls.

It makes us dance
It makes us sing
as it rocks and it rolls.

But every record
comes to an end
and so does this poem.
In my heart
and in my soul
sweet music will always have a home.

A rather silly little ditty. Nearly Doctor Seuss-like. It's pretty self-explanatory. Leave it to music to end up being the inspiration for one of my longest poems ever. Music has always been such an important part of my life. My passion for music is absolutely boundless. Since I graduated High School, I have been involved in music *somehow* my entire adult life.

Be it singing in a band, having my own afternoon drive-time radio request show on a medium-market share FM adult contemporary radio station, Djing in huge Nightclubs and Bottle clubs, even hosting a local parade in my town for 9 years as an MC and DJ. I have also spent decades working on the *other* side of the spotlight as a stage hand, Lighting Designer/Director and Master Production Electrician. As you can guess, I have spent *most* of my life holding down more than one job at once.

And please, PLEASE don't come at me in defense of Hip-Hop. My opinions about that current state of affairs are absolute. Actually, I have toured with SNAP!, Wu Tang Clan, Method Man and Red Man, Onyx, Bone-Thugs & Harmony and have worked with nearly EVERY Hip Hop artist you could EVER name as a Lighting Director in my 35 years in the "Biz". I even worked for Russell Simmons as the Lighting Director of the Def Jam 10th Anniversary Tour.

As for "Street Cred", I LIVED at Park and Broadway Brooklyn for almost 8 years, right across Park Ave. from The Sumner Houses projects in Bed-Stuy. So, don't DREAM of challenging me about "what I know" about Hip Hop or having street cred. To polish all that, I was a nightclub DJ for 20 years. Chances are, I was spinning "White Lines" in a late night bottle club or roller skating to "Rappers Delight" BEFORE your parents even MET! I DO love much of the current stuff ... Some of these new artists write challenging, very spiritual and moving lyrics!

BUT ...

SO, SO much of it is complete and utter GARBAGE. The violence, crime and misogyny that it glorifies is so far beyond belligerent, ignorant AND pathetic. In my opinion, it takes the listeners all *backwards,* instead of projecting them forward. It seems to me, that after 'Buffalo Stance" ... it all started going downhill ... *most* of it, anyway.

Challenging me about this would be like trying to tackle a red brick wall. Your words will fall on Def Ears ... (PUN INTENDED)

My Top 10 Albums (The one's I'd HAVE to have if stranded on a desert island), in no certain order, as I love them all the same, with no certain favorite:

Johnny Cash – Unearthed

The Black Crowes – Southern Harmony and Musical Companion

Led Zeppelin - The Song Remains The Same

The Beastie Boys – Licensed To Ill

Tori Amos – Under The Pink

Company Of Thieves – Ordinary Riches

Rage Against The Machine – Live at the Grand Olympic Auditorium (Japanese Import version)

Pink Floyd - Animals

Madonna – Ray Of Light

Bob Marley & The Wailers – Babylon By Bus

U2 – The Joshua Tree

The Fugees – The Score

Willie Nelson – 16 Greatest Hits

Pink Floyd – Pulse (Vinyl Edition)

The Crystal Method – Vegas

25 Years of Motown #1 Hits – A multi-artist, multi disc, collection of Motown Music from the 50's, 60's, and 70's

The Beatles – Revolver

SNAP! - World Power

Allman Brothers Band – Eat A peach (2006 Deluxe version)

The Blues Brothers – The Complete Blues Brothers

Bare Naked Ladies – Rock Spectacle

The Complete Woodstock Recording

(For those of you that *CAN'T* count … that's actually 22! (I snuck the extra ones onto the island on a thumb drive hidden in my sock!) … and *yes* … I *love* live music! (Go figure)

I know, I know, dear Reader … "Thumb Drive … On a desert island?"

Yo, my book … my parameters. Besides … the music *has* to be on *SOME* type of media!

Don't like it?

Then write yourself onto your *OWN* damn desert island and sneak your *own* flippin' music!

And while I'm at it … I think I'll tuck another drive in my other sock with all of my board and bootleg tape collection on it! Stage Hands and Road Dogs collect and trade recordings of bands given to us by the Front of House Mixers or Bootleggers. (It's an insider thing.)

Amoung some of my favs? Train in Atlanta, Pink Floyd Tour Rehearsals from Miami, Fiona Apple in Phoenix, Depeche Mode in Paris, Cyndi Lauper in Chicago, The Rolling Stones in Gainesville, Fugees at the Nassau Coliseum, Deep Purple in Berlin, Lou Reed at Highline Ballroom, Peaches at Highline Ballroom, Buju Banton at Reggae SumFest in Jamaica, U2 in London, Rush in Toronto, and a Jam Band taper's recording of the Allman Brothers live at the Beacon Theater.

(Eat your hearts out)

Stubborn

When I was young, I was told
that I could be whatever I wish.
But I have learned it's not always true
Be you a man
A dog
Or a fish.

I worked my fingers to the bone.
On me, the boss could depend.
He got rich.
And what did I get?
Torn clothes,
Sore back,
Split ends.

Some employees get ahead.
Now this I know to be true.
But if you look beyond,
I think you'll find
That their biggest dreams fell through.

Happiness is relative,
I guess.
Where ever you go,
You are.
But losing a dream just for comfort?
'Tis the most common crime, by far.

I will stay
In the ring.
Battered.
Surely bruised.
I will never let go of my dreams
and never ever be used.

I want the world to know my name
And my words,
To make others richer.
So that when I step out

through these ropes,
all will emerge a victor.

And if I should leave it
in some other style,
it is still not a loss.
I did things
the way that I believed
and I
was always the boss.

At least I'll know that I tried.

I'm really proud of the whimsy in this. I think it's the Irish in my veins, trying to toss a limerick!

My Cup Runneth Over

Now I've been told
That I can be
As mean as a bull.

And if you hand a cup to me,
It'd damn well better be full.

If I pour my self over you,
If it's your cup I fill …
And you don't fill me back up again,
Tell me then . . . who will?

Time fly's by,
Even pain can pass.

But no one that I've ever met,
Likes an empty glass.

Now I've been told
That you can be
As stubborn as a mule.

But if you wish to play some game with me,
You'd damn well not play me a fool.

If I pour my heart out for you,
If I give you more than enough,
You can't just give me nothing back
And tell me "Oh, that's tough"

'Cause time fly's by
And even pain can pass.

But not a soul that roams this earth,
Likes an empty glass.

CCXXXIX

My last 6 vehicles have been: 4 pickup trucks and 2 vans. I like the convenience of being able to drive nearly anywhere and to be able to haul and move stuff. It's the utilitarian in me, I guess. One thing you *must* accept when owning this type of vehicle is that you WILL be asked to help folks move stuff. Be it a couch, a dresser or even a whole house during a move ... the requests *will* come.

I had done this countless times. But once, when I was moving a whole house, I couldn't believe how some of the folks I had so readily helped were suddenly "too busy" to help me ... offering up a plethora of reasons. What made me mad, was later finding out that most of their *excuses* were Bull$4#t!

Face Up

Leaving the clinic
Wishing to be a cynic.
But I believe
What he's told me
And now ... I have to "live" with it.

Sit in the truck, my hands are shaking.
I'm trying to escape the sense that it's making.
How can this be?
It is happening to me.
No choice ... I have to "live" with it.

Round two sweeps my mind.
I could never, ever, be so unkind.
To have a woman
    fall in love with me
Only to leave them
    sad, in pain ... empty.
So alone ... I'll have to "live" with it.

Like both cheeks smacked, a painful sting.
A given time limit and no woman for my ring.
No pitter patter will ever wake me
      in the middle of the night.
No more other halves to ever show me
      new kinds of light.
Now accepting ... I have to "live" with it.

Stoic I stand ... Stoic I will stay.
I'm far too proud to face this any other way.
No more broken hearts for me, at least ...
      and lots of places that I want to see.
I'll be an even better man now, I know ...
     than I've ever tried to be.
Because now ... I have to "live" with it.

Sad as it may be … Sometimes bad news can actually make you an even better person.

I wrote this in 2005, the moment I got home from the clinic … where the Doctor there had informed me that I had " … the lungs of an 80 year old man", had chronic COPD and that I had "six to ten years to live". I had told him to "Give it to me straight" … *But* … I honestly didn't expect all that. To tell you this was soul shaking does not even begin to express the emotions I experienced that Fall afternoon.

I had noticed feeling out of breath after carrying out a large bag of trash. This made me pay more attention and then realized I was seemingly out of shape. But … I shouldn't have been. I was still in top form, working long hours on stagehand gigs and never batting an eye. I could go 7 am 'til 1-2 am and then drive 2 hours home from Orlando.

Easy-peasy.

I could go 24 hours on a stadium steel show set-up gig, then go home, sleep 8 hours and be back to do the entire show day (changing bands, etc.), which included loading out the show *and then* the steel … *non-stop*. Heh, some of the twenty-somethings couldn't do this and I was in my early forties! I was also going boating and out on other adventures with my buds … doing all the things I had always done. But now, I found myself panting, when I shouldn't have been. It was quite unnerving.

I decided to see a doctor and get checked out. One test led to another and another … blowing in tubes, floating little balls in tubes and several x-rays as well. That final consultation really took me down several pegs. I simply couldn't believe it. But in my truck, in the clinic parking lot and all the way to my driveway …

I had many realizations … epiphany's … many things I knew that I now had to accept … and I also summed up many things that I wanted to do and see while I still could. The biggest thing … was the realization that I could *never* have another steady girlfriend. That one was hard. At that moment, I wasn't with anyone.

I knew that I could *never* go and have some poor girl fall in love with me, all the while knowing she would have to watch me die. It just isn't in me to do that to someone. It's just wrong. So, realizing I would face this problem, *and* the rest of my life, alone came like a wave over my head.

It was the hardest realization I'd ever had, next to learning my condition ... and *both* came in the span of fifteen minutes.

Taking stock in who is important among your family and friends is not something you ever picture yourself doing. You just kinda take those things as they come. After being given a time limit, you think about a lot of things you'd never thought of before. Prioritizing things, becomes a way of life.

That's why I moved to China.

That's why I moved to NYC.

I wanted to experience those things before my time came.

I didn't tell anyone, not even my family, until over 11 years later. I didn't want anyone looking at me like they *"knew"* ... friends *or* family ... it would have been more than I could bare. Besides, why put them though that? I'm a very proud person.

On top of that ... I didn't want anyone giving me "passes" or pity because they knew I was sick. That would just make me angry ... not at them, per se ... at my situation. I enjoy proving myself and earning my own way. I just really wanted to deal with this on my own and on my own terms. I wanted to see and experience things I'd dreamed of all my life but never took the time to pursue.

Really ...

How silly is it that it took this kind of news to motivate me to do the things I'd dreamed of?

As you can see, I have outlived his time limit. I'm doing okay. I also openly talk about it. It is what it is. I'm doing the best that I can. I have since been dealt some other health issues; have gone on Disability and I fight for my health every day. Some days are better than others.

After the Elvis Costello Tour, things took a turn for the worse. My legs were stiffening by simply walking to the J train. I'd have to stop two or three times between home and work. After a flight of stairs up to, or out of, the subway, I would feel like I'd carried a thousand-pound gorilla up those steps. Knowing that I had gone past my ten year time limit, I assumed that my time was coming.

I went to a walk-in clinic on 14th Street. I passed it all the time. After examining me, the Doctor looked a bit pale ... My heart sunk ... He told me to go straight to the emergency room and "... Get your lower body examined for clots". He wouldn't touch me ... he wouldn't even *charge* me ...

That ... made *me* go pale.

I mean ... how bad of a condition do you have to be in for a Doctor, in New York City, no less ... to tell you "No Charge" as he urges you from his clinic to a hospital emergency room?

It was nearly as soul shredding as the first trip to the clinic in Florida 12 years before ... all over again.

After several X-rays, the Doctors in the hospital he had sent me to told me that I had collapsing/hardening veins in my legs as well as mild blockages, not clots ... so, I just assumed the worst. It all sounded to me like it was part of my existing condition, so when they wanted to make appointments for me to see a Doctor about treatments, I didn't want to waste the money.

I just figured that I already knew what was happening. I made the assumption that there wasn't much I could do about it. So, I honestly went home to be with my family ... and die.

I just wanted to spend my last days with them. I'd seen them only once in nearly ten years.

But when I went to new Doctors there in Alabama while applying for the Disability, they explained that surgery could open my veins back up. It was a common affliction for folks my age. The shortness of breath that was now coming with near any exertion was because those veins were starving my heart for blood. It *wasn't* my COPD.

That didn't *help*, but it wasn't the actual cause.

All I needed was stents. I hadn't gotten to that phase with the NYC Docs, I just assumed the worst and left NYC. When I got to my family, I was so bad that I couldn't work or afford the surgeries. So I applied for disability and am now, with the help of Medicare, getting the surgeries.

I have faced so much in these last thirteen years since that first trip to the clinic...

But no matter what ... I will *not* go without a fight.

I am *still* trying to get the current stuff cleared up enough to get back out on the road. Touring is something I really love. I'm also not one to just lay down and take government handouts. I went on Disability for the Medicare. I'm hoping that the Stents and other stuff I need to get back out there will do the trick. Then I can go off of Disability and do what I love. Maybe ... *hopefully* ... by the time you read this ... I may have all that underway.

To hell with a time limit. I'll live until I don't. I don't dwell on it. After outliving this time limit like this, I have a new-found gumption to just press on, the way I've always done.

Hell ... What else *can* you do?

The COPD still makes things tough. I hate my inhaler because the steroids in it make my tongue swell and then I bite it in my sleep.

Ugh.

I only use it when the breathing gets really bad.

And ya know what, dear Reader?

The new Doctors wont give you a time limit any more ...

They reserve that for people with dire, immediate terminal illnesses. They also have said that they don't do that anymore *because* of people like me ...

Good for me.

Exaspiraspiration

There is this place I love to go,
some would call it a dream.
I smile and laugh with all who're there,
no one is ever mean.

It's not one place I drift off to ...
It changes all the time.
The same location, night and day,
would truly dull the mind.

Exploring the seas
and mountains
and caves.
Zooming low
over high tree tops
and skimming across the waves.

It's not a delusion of grandeur
nor a proclamation of emancipation ...
It's really more like a form of
therapeutic anticipation.

It's not that I hate being here,
I simply aspire to do more.
I have so much to share with the world
and places I wish to explore.

Share is the watchword here.
I want something back.
I wish to see and do and learn ...
To gain the things that I lack.

But somewhere here along the way, something's bogged me down.
I find myself spinning my wheels and often wearing frowns.

I close my eyes and off I go, to the place I've told you about ...
I see it more like a vacation ... *not* a desperate way out.

I'm sure one morning that I'll wake up
and I'll be there for real.

Then no more moments of my day,
on this journey will I have to steal.

This was written a very long time ago at a moment in my life when I was feeling exasperated and frustrated about all my efforts seeming to end up fruitless. We all go there sooner or later, don't we?

I think I was in my early 30's and getting a lot of rejection emails on my first Novel. My writing was doing great online, my poetry winning awards ...

My favorite part of it is the multi-syllable words strung together. I was just beginning to stretch my wings with whimsy and wordsmithing.

But, without a degree, the "Literati" in the publishing world will usually have little or nothing to do with you. To them, I guess ... without that paper, how could you POSSIBLY have something to write about?

Now ... *soooo* many years later ... they are being proven so, so wrong by amazing writers that do *not* have college degree's. I'm not kicking college, by any means ... but God bless the internet *and* Amazon!

This is just simply one of things we write as a form of "self-medication" as-it-were. It did make me feel better ... and as it always does ... things got better.

Such a Roller Coaster we are all riding, huh?!

Arsenal

There are so many weapons that we can choose …
to make others suffer or to bring them pain.

There's double-edged swords and
the ol' forked tongue … Why, endless badgering …
can surely drive one insane.

There's guns of all calibers,
shanks and dirks, even poison's galore.

The mighty pen or the dangled noose,
a shove off a cliff and so, so many more to explore …

But there is one …

Thee simplest, yet most painful, of all.

You needn't lift a finger …
Ne'er spend one dime … You surely won't make a call.

You see, it takes all but zero effort or practice …
and it requires absolutely zero science.

No weapon in the Arsenal can make one suffer …
quite as horribly as silence.

My thoughts on the pain of being shut out or ignored.

I Dare ...

I'll tell you,
It's great to be different.

I love to swim upstream.

I must often settle for lesser joys,
But I never cease to dream.

In
Through the out door,

Running
Up that hill.

I may sit down to rest sometimes.

But I never,

Ever

Sit still.

Up all night

Or up all day ...

I may not care what you think,
But I respect it in every way.

I don't expect you to see the world
Looking through my eyes.

I do,

However,

Expect you to

Share with me
The sky.

Born In a barn,
Born in a Jeep
Or born with a silver spoon.
We roam this place,
CCLI

Together

Or not

And we all need a little room.

I do as I please.

I speak my mind.

This
will always be so.

I dare
To be me . . .

And I do it wherever I go.

Imagine a world,
Honest and real.

To thine own self, be true.

I rarely ever
Wear a mask . . .

Now ask yourself,
Do you?

I was sitting at my local pub watching a Steelers game (or was it the Bucs?) and I got mad at a Ref's call against my team. In anger, I took the napkin in my hand and balled it up and threw it at the TV screen before even realizing what I had done. BIG no-no ... no matter *where* you are. *Especially* a sports bar!

Impulsive?

You bet.

Childish?

Of course ... But that's me sometimes.

The Manager, Phil, a pal of mine, laughed at me and chastised me at the same time. Later, he told me: "You know what I love about you Jeffy? No matter where you are ... you are always yourself. I've *never* seen you change ... *anywhere* we are. It takes guts to just be you, especially with such a strong personality." Before he said that to me ... I had *never* given it much thought.

Starlight

I dreamed
that I was starlight

Drifting
Here and there …

in a bliss-full void
without bounds …
where time didn't care.

It smelled wonderful.
It tasted sweet.
It didn't matter why.

A peaceful deep,
Fulfilling breath …
Contentment with a sigh.

All I've seen …
All I've done …
My experiences … the thread …

Not of my life, as a whole …
but the path by which I've led.

I saw the lesson that was this dream …
My life … the vast expanse.

The thread was true as it made its way …
not one stitch by chance.

It matters not who I've been… nor what I've been through.
Ne'er meant to change whom we are …
Only what we do.

I wrote this, in my bed one morning, after awaking from the oddest dream I'd ever had. Over a decade later, I wrote something that expounded on this after letting it sink in a bit deeper, titled "Celestial".

CCLV

Restless

My soul was meant to be still
And my soul was meant to talk.
My soul was meant to listen and
My soul was meant to walk.

My soul has been filled to the brim with laughter
And my soul has soared in the sky.
My soul has climbed deep underground and
My soul has been known to sigh.

My soul has shared so many lives
And they've touched me, every one.
My soul has left with them each a piece
And still, it's never done.

My soul has wandered through mountains
And my soul has slept on the sea.
My soul is almost always content
And yet,
My soul wonders where it should be.

My soul was meant to be searching
And my soul has shared its mind.
My soul has been the student and
My soul was meant to find.

My soul has played the gallant host
And it has been the thankful guest.
My soul never knows where it will be and
It never seems to rest.

And though it never knows where it will be,
My soul is never lost.
My soul has been living an incredible life
And it pays an incredible cost.

The trade off must be fair though,
My soul is as happy as can be.
I'm prone to exaggeration some,
But hey then, that's just me.

My soul has lived a life unbound
And yet,
My soul has yearned for a home.
My soul,
Like a leaf
That's let go of the vine,
On the wind is cheerfully blown.

I wrote this in my early 30's as I began to realize the fact that I wasn't married with children and that my life was seemingly on a different course of globetrotting with bands and doing shows and interactions with many, many people. Not what I'd always imagined ... and yet, I felt a strange contentment.

Perhaps, it was also me accepting myself on another, or the "next", level, if you will. I have always been comfortable with myself and who I am. Even when finding, or seeing myself in new lights or on paths I hadn't imagined being on.

I once read a quote from Madonna, where she had been asked by a fan or reporter or whomever:

"Why do you always take the hard road?"

Her response, to me, was priceless and I *totally* identified with it ...

She replied simply: "What makes you think I see a road?"

Most folks are bombarded by their family and the outside world to "buckle down" ... "Be successful" ... etc. etc. And doing that is a perfectly acceptable thing to do. Bless you.

It is both honorable and respectable.

But who is to say that living a comfortable life of gathering experiences is unacceptable? It would seem to me that that would be someones morals or standards being projected on someone else. No matter how you look at that, it is wrong. I've often yearned for my own home and family ... but it does not mean that I *miss* those things.

It is what it is.

Also, I'm not talking about folks that live at home sponging off of their parents or their families refusing to get or keep a job all their lives. THAT ... is just pathetic and lazy. A life wasted away ... centered on selfishness and self-entitlement. Professional *losers*.

I'm talking about looking after yourself and enjoying an exciting life filled with travel and adventure. You might have a myriad of jobs along the way. Or maybe you only have one. But just because you don't own a bunch of nice things or have the security of your own home or family, does *not* mean that you are "unsuccessful".

In my humble opinion ... it simply means that you have *lived*.

The Sky

I wish the sky would make up its mind
as I search for the things
I'm hoping to find.

A tightrope walk
over a dark abyss.
Sometimes I hit,
sometimes I miss.

From the mountains to the desert,
the sky is the same.
But, sometimes it's sunshine
and sometimes it's rain.

Up so high ... Oh so down ...
Sometimes I thirst.
Sometimes I drown.

Rivers flood ... dust blows away.
Sometimes it's night.
Sometimes it's day

Clouds so dark ... Snow so white.
Sometimes I'm serene
and sometimes ... I fight.

So ironic ... the future ... built by the past.
I guess it's true ...
nothing gold can last.

Thunder and lightning.
Cool windy shade.
Sometimes I swim
and sometimes ... I wade.

Sometimes there's stars ... Sometimes a moon.
I hope that I find what I'm looking for ... soon.

But, it's not only gold ...
I've been hoping to find.
I just wish the sky ...
would make up its mind.

Based on the idiom: "Out of the clear blue sky".

I had been going through SO many things at the time I wrote this. I was trying to get my house and property together so that I could open my own Nursery and Gardens Business. I planned on having a small Nursery with plants and flowers, as well as breeding and selling Koi Fish. I was also going to design and install nice gardens in folk's back yards for them to enjoy and hang out in.

But, it seemed, every time I completed a task, I had to then do two or three more ... *or* ... I would discover that in order to do one task, I first had to first complete two or three others!

On our way to my truck to go and do yet another newly found task, a pal of mine and I were joking about the never-ending to-do list. During this period, as is typical in Florida, the weather kept changing. This too, was sometimes holding up getting some of the tasks finished and in frustration, I blurted out: "Yes ... I just wish the sky would make up its mind", meant as a double entendre about the weather *and* all the seemingly self-multiplying tasks.

The whole way to Home Depot, and all the way back, this poem formed itself in my head. Before we could unload the truck, I had to run inside and drop it on my 'puter.

Monster

I know that I'm a monster …
and to the world, I look like one.
Big and tall, with long, wild hair
and a shadow that can block out the sun.

Yes, I know I'm a monster.
Strong, cunning and fierce.
My hands have done extensive destruction
and my stare has been known to pierce.

But these are only capabilities.
That is not who I am.
I'm actually the nicest guy you've ever met.
A kind and gentle man.

I love children, flowers and animals.
I love all things beautiful … and smiles.
My heart has been described as bigger than the Moon …
and loving … all the while.

I love to plan, design and create.
Yes, I can be extremely constructive.
I've commanded crews of over fifty people
and alone, been very productive.

My work ethic is second to none.
I'm honest and true to the cause.
I'm dependable, thoughtful and trustworthy …
ever trying to mend my own flaws.

If you call upon me to do a task,
rest assured that it will be done …
and if there's a bully or bad guy around
my monster will make them run.

Yes, I know I'm a monster.
But that's only one thing that I can be.
He only comes out when he is needed.
The rest of the time … I'm me.

I spent nearly 8 years living in Bed-Stuy Brooklyn. Park Ave. and Broadway. Right across the street from the Sumner Houses section. People died on my block at a rate of one or so a month. 4 different times, I heard the actual shots that I would later learn had taken the lives of people. I heard gun fire and/or screaming on a nearly nightly basis.

Daytime was okay.

But at *night* ... all bets were off.

In the entire time that I lived there, I walked the streets coming home from the train and bars and even work, as late as 3-4 in the morning. NOT ONCE was I ever accosted or even approached, let alone hurt or robbed. *Several* folks from my building had had *both* happen to them over the years I was there.

Aside from the Angel that has apparently been living upon my shoulder for most all of my life ... I accredit this uncanny security to the outward appearance I have been bestowed with. I am a big guy, 6 foot tall, 275 pounds, long curly brown hair, a mustache and soul patch. I have a cocky, confident swagger when I walk, always with my head up and always taking in my surroundings.

I've come to the conclusion that the bad guys take one look at me and then ponder: "Ehhh, let's just wait on the next one."

Remedium

I write these words to heal my heart
and all the hurt in my chest.
Though in sorrow,
I pen them with strength,
my only wish …
to put everything to rest.

I write these lines to heal my soul …
untying the knots with each and every verse.
Though in pain,
I craft them with love
and hope …
to feel better …
when things surely can't get any worse.

A bit of introspection on my part. Redundant, I guess … writing a poem about writing "therapeutic" poems for my own self-healing. But … there it is.

The Dead of Winter

The leaves …
dead,
have all turned brown.

Once …
green in the wind,
now scattered upon the ground.

The branches …
bare,
like cold aching bones.

They creak and whistle
in that wind …
lonely and alone.

The air …
silent,
all wings having fled for the sun.

Skies and forests once filled …
now empty.
Not a stir to be heard … not even one.

Snow …
barren
as a desert without life.

Water has become like stone,
as is a man
without a wife.

Monochrome vistas … everywhere you gaze.
Ethereal …
like this swirling mist that is my very breath.

Peaceful, stark beauty …
found only during Winter …
standing in stoic contempt … of all its magnific death.

A bit of a cryptic/metaphorical piece.

It is about the things I've seen during winter. But I've taken those elements and scenes and metaphorically turned them into elements of myself and my life ...

My accomplishments and experiences, my inner self, my friends and family, even my heart ... and how I can still be strong and even content as I enter this time ... still finding beauty in it all while facing the winter of my life.

On Being You

Enemy Mine …

"In his book "The Art of War", Sun Tzu teaches:

"If you know the enemy and know yourself, you need not fear the result of a hundred battles. If you know yourself but not the enemy, for every victory gained you will also suffer a defeat. If you know neither the enemy nor yourself, you will succumb in every battle."

I could not agree with this philosophy or this teaching more. It does make perfect sense … *Still* … I've often learned from experience that sometimes … the *real* enemy **is** *you*.

I've read this passage a thousand times and have yet to figure out whether this was actually what he was saying … *or* … did he miss that completely? Knowing ones self doesn't necessarily mean you can see yourself as the enemy … that you recognize that *you* are the one whom is actually holding yourself back.

I think Oscar Wilde said it best, when he wrote: *"We are each our own devils … and we make this world our living hell"*. It is mind boggling how we can simply torture ourselves sometimes with goals, expectations, and self-imposed morals and values … or even worse … when we allow ourselves to either have them dictated to us by others or we blindly follow their expectations to "fit in" or be accepted. Many of these things, self-inflicted or otherwise, are either patently unobtainable or simply unrealistic

Why do we do this to ourselves?

I think it is because we are humans.

As such, we have an internal *need* to be accepted *and* the unlimited ability to dream …

Our imaginations are absolutely boundless.

Our dreams can be simply fantastical.

But … *sometimes*, we have nightmares in our sleep …

The problem is … subconsciously … inexplicably … instead of dreams … we can, and do sometimes, impose waking nightmares upon ourselves."

~Jeff Gaines

Sonder

If you only look for the bad in people,
You will let the good ones slip by.
Someone that would do anything for you,
without ever asking you why.

There really is true good left in the world.
I see it every day.
It may be a favor, a smile or a door held open.
It comes in so many ways.

Not every one that you encounter
is a liar or a thief or a hater.
But if you don't even give them at least half a chance,
you'll just never know, neither now nor later.

Trust is something that you must do with a friend,
just as you do with a lover.
You must show your neck for them to see and reach,
lest you might never discover.

This offer of vulnerability is a test,
that they can kiss, bite or ignore.
But if you don't expose it, in fear or in doubt,
your quest for love turns to endless chore.

Perhaps … it is you who are bad …
so, you are convinced that all others must be.
But that is something you must ask of yourself,
just look in your heart and see.

But if you are good, then take that chance,
the rewards may never end.
There is nothing, not anything, as great an asset
as that of having a friend.

I'm not saying don't watch for the bad.
In fact, I never would.
I'm saying that if you only look for that …
You will never find the good.

The original title of this poem was "Sentient".

After learning the meaning and concept of "Sonder", I found it was a far and away better title. There is a talented girl on Hello poetry with the handle "Sondering". She is from the Philippines.

After enjoying some of her poetry and chatting a bit through messages, I decided to look up what that meant, as I could tell that it wasn't a proper name and I was too shy to ask her. I was fascinated by what I found:

~SONDER - n. the realization that each random passerby is living a life as vivid and complex as your own.

Find it here: https://en.wiktionary.org/wiki/sonder

Open The Window

Every office should have a window
and so should every mind.
Without a view on the world outside
a soul will simply go blind.

All work and no play
will make a mind go dim.
Never seeing the world and those around you
will certainly collapse you within.

Taking in a soothing view
or seeing someone to help in need …
keeps the mind … and the heart
from letting darkness breed.

The light that comes through these windows
imagined or very real …
lifts the soul on multiple levels and
gives us the passion to feel.

So, open the window that you have there …
on the wall or in your mind.
Enjoy the breeze and scent of the flowers
and to others, show them you're kind.

If you practice these things with your windows ...
in all that you say and do …
You'll always carry a window for your spirit …
and its view that you saw through.

This poem was inspired by the Company of Thieves song "Window".

It may not be about the same things that Genevieve was expressing, but it was the inspiration, nonetheless.

Such a moving and beautiful song.

I hope that they don't mind.

Stipulatio (The Contract)

When you say "I love you",
you've made a contract with a heart.
It's a tangible thing, very real …
and binding, right from the start.

It states that you'll be there,
steady and true …
your colors never fading
or even changing hue.

You've declared that this heart means something
to the one that beats in your chest.
You've sworn to be faithful and willing
to always give only your best.

But so many souls
carelessly throw those words around.
They are just so easy to say.

When spoken insincerely,
they leave hearts on the ground.
Such a terrible price to pay.

Will you contemplate this agreement, deep in your mind,
before you sign this page?

Of course! This mise is for two souls to fly together
and never for one to be caged.

And how will keep your promise to be there,
bringing laughs and fending fears?

With hugs and encouragement to warm that heart,
a friend throughout the years.

Must you remember your covenant?

Oh yes … forever seeing it through.

Must you keep your honor and never break it?

Of this, be sure … as you'd not want that done to you.

(BTW, of course, this word is Latin)

From Wikipedia: "Stipulatio was the basic form of a contract in Roman law. It was made in the format of question and answer."

This is a slightly rewritten version from the one that appeared on Hello Poetry. I took the 6th and 7th verses and converted them to be question and answer, in order to be more "in the theme" of the title.

For Ethereal ...

" ... And I dress this way just to keep them at bay,
'cause Halloween is every day!"
-Al Jourgenson
From the 1984 Ministry Title: "Everyday (is Halloween)"

Masks are good sometimes.

We're taught to wear them since childhood.

One for our parents ...

One for our teacher ...

One for our friends ...

Even one for our Preacher!

It's when we can't be without one ...
that something is wrong.

When we can't take them off ...
that our identity is gone.

Fear can make us want to leave them on ...
and sometimes it can be shame.

But ...
if you ask the person behind the mask ...

I'd bet ...
they blame the pain.

I was chatting online with a girl I'd met in some Yahoo Chat room, her online handle was "Ethereal". We were chatting about how we all wear masks for different reasons, it is a natural defense mechanism, after all. We chatted about how it can be helpful or even "politically correct" for a given situation and how that it can also sometimes be problematic or even damaging to ourselves and those around us.

I read what I had just typed and couldn't believe it, I didn't mean to make it rhyme, I swear … it just came out that way. I cut and pasted it into MSWord, separated and stacked it into verses and made it into this piece, ver batum.

Oddly, that happened again in another online chat (though that one did not rhyme). It became "Searcher". So funny … so odd, how some of my writings come about.

Adding the Ministry quote came to me as I reread the piece the first few times. It reminded me of the song. It was one of my favorite songs from that era, a Goth anthem, and its subject was a perfect marriage to the piece, showing that entire groups of people wear masks, in one form or another, as a way of life … for reasons that they see as completely normal.

At one moment or another … don't we all?

Tools

If you should decide to collect people as tools,
for your own purpose … or just for fun …
you have to be wary … lest you will find,
you've garnered every type under the sun.

Some do their job.
Some come with a crew.
Some come completely broken and …
some will be working you.

Some work perfectly,
tasking without a peep.
Some bring grief and headaches
with no morals or standards to keep.

Some come with outstretched arms
and some with outstretched hands …
Either may be disarming veils of deception.

You may never notice though,
as your focus upon yourself
keenly clouds your perception.

The next thing you know …
they have ruined your goal.
If particularly cruel …
even damaged your soul.

With smiles and hugs,
just like yours … seemingly right from the heart …
they can steal your coins and your wishes …
and they'll do it right from the start.

And just as you swapped them out for newer,
more useful tools …
Some will see through you and disappear …
so as not to be used as fools.

As time goes on, there's a lesson to be learned …
and yet some never grasp it, it seems …

CCLXXIX

These tools, in your toolbox aren't tools at all …
They are people *… with lives and hopes and dreams …*
just like you.

Be careful and be NICE!

That's the only advice I can give when practicing this behavior. We are *all* guilty of it at some time or another … in some form, or another. Hell, some folks are highly skilled professionals at it!

But being "pals" with the guy at the Theater snack bar because he hooks you up with free butter on your popcorn is one thing … using someone for rides without paying for gas or getting someone to do your work while you take the credit is a whole other animal.

Such an odd behavior, this … using other people as a tool. In nature, it happens all the time. For instance, there are "cleaning fish" called "Wrasse" on reefs that many sea creatures use to clean off dead skin and other parasites.

The wrasse get a free meal and even protection from their "clients". These types of "tool" behaviors are beneficial for all. There are also species that lay eggs upon or even inside a "host". When the larvae hatch, they consume the host, most often leading to death. Obviously, being *that* kind of tool is not beneficial for the tool.

We too, can have these types of "tools" … as they can be beneficial, or detrimental, for us as well. Sometimes we can offer ourselves up as tools. Even if it's only offering them an ear or some friendly company now and then.

Or perhaps taking out the elderly neighbor ladies trash now and then. If she bakes you a pie or watches your kids for an hour, then all is in balance. If they cherish the symbiosis, regardless of what form it comes in, then they benefit as well.

But the other end of that spectrum in the animal world is the parasite. I needn't explain that … *OR* show the comparison to their human counterparts!

What If?

What if we were all born blind?

Would it matter then what we wear?

I mean, if we had no eyes with which to see,
We'd then have none to stare.

What if we were all born deaf?

Would it matter then what we heard?

I mean, if we had no ears with which to listen,
We'd then not hear a word.

And what if we were all born without a heart?

Would it matter then how we feel?

I mean, if we had no soul with which to love,
How could anything be real?

What if . . .
Nothing is real?

Just in case you are wondering ... I wrote this over a decade *before* "The Matrix" movie franchise debuted. I did think about it and grin as I watched the first installment. But, the two have nothing whatsoever to do with each other ... except maybe coincidence, at best.

Horology

Clawing your way out of the mud, rising above the clouds,
wanting the best for others
or washing off the grime ...
Always remember that having
a real hope, is never a waste of time.

Someone that knows all about you, still standing by your side,
letting you help when they need it
or sharing a bottle of wine ...
You mustn't forget that befriending
a real friend, is never a waste of time.

Seeing a better way, wishing upon on a star,
aspiring to a better life
or surpassing the paradigm ...
Don't ever lose faith that dreaming
a real dream, is never a waste of time.

Head back, loud and boisterous or hidden behind your hand,
giggling at a friends comical tragedy
or a surprisingly witty punch line ...
Take great joy in knowing that laughing
a real laugh, is never a waste of time.

That friend in need, the stranger with a flat in the rain,
the little sister with the broken doll,
or the old couple with health in decline ...
The gift you give by lending
a real hand, is never a waste of time.

The warm feeling of being wanted, knowing someone cares,
finding someone that shares their soul with you,
a faithful partner in crime ...
Let your heart find solace that loving
a real love, is never a waste of time.

Teaching a child to color, a puppy to chase a ball,
being enthralled watching a hummingbird
or soothed by a soft wind chime ...

Find contentment in knowing that enjoying
a real life, in everything that you do …
is never, ever a waste of time.

"ho·rol·o·gy"
hə'räləjē
noun
The study and measurement of time.

I have to make a confession, dear Reader … I have a fetish. Now, get your mind out of the gutter and let me explain …

I _LOVE_ watches!

Especially hand-built Swiss watches. Especially skeletonized watches that let you see all that unbelievable craftsmanship. I don't wear or even own any jewelry … But … I _do_ own 8 watches at this writing. I'm just fascinated with the design and skill set that goes into making hand-made watches. I can't afford the real-deal Swiss watches … my goodness, they _start_ at like $3000.00 for "entry-level" watches like Brietling's and Rolex's and can go up into the _millions_!

Most of my watches are automatics, but I do have a few purist, self or hand-winding, mechanical watches and a few vintage pieces as well. A person that shares my fetish, whether they collect watches or clocks or whatever is called a "Horologist" … I _am_ one of _those_.

I got to thinking about that term and the study of time in general. I pondered it all day one day (I know, I'm _such_ a weirdo) and I thought about how we pass through time "doing" things. There is no better way to put it. Be it sleeping or writing or driving or playing solitaire or mowing the lawn … we are constantly doing things.

We put such an importance on our "precious time". It has been expressed by everyone in some way or another. We value our time. It can be well spent, searched for, given away, bought and even wasted. It is a tangible thing that you can _NOT_ hold in your hand.

Mystical indeed.

Think about it …

That being said, I got home from driving around in town running errands and when I sat down at my 'puter, I opened MSWord and typed "Horology" at the top of the page.

What spilled out after that is what you see here. I realize that its structure and format are a bit odd … even for me. It's nearly a mash-up of poetry and spoken word. But I do love the way it came together.

It was a lovely way to pass the time.

Celestial

You can never use the superficial to dismiss or disguise the supernatural.
This task will prove ever impossible.
The answer to ... The reality that is ... The truth about ... The solution for ...
everything ... does not just dwell within you ...

It *is* you.

All you have seen.
All you have done.
All of the laughs you've ever had.
Every tear that you have ever cried.
All of the pains that you have ever endured.
All of the joy that you have ever experienced.
All of the things that you have ever been ... to anyone.
Every single thing that has ever been done for you ... *or to you.*
Each and every moment that you have *ever* lived ... both light *and* dark ...
has bestowed upon you every strength that you will *ever* need.

These experiences make up the very essence of you ... Your blessed soul.
All you have to do is recognize it and accept it *all.*
Only then, will it empower you.

Your soul is celestial. You can not transform something of divine existence ...
nor can you make any moment of its life
ever go away ... they exist *for* you.
Putting a mask on it or hiding from any one moment, defeats their very purpose.

Embracing your soul, *as is,* might seem the most frightening thing that you'll ever
do ... *but* ... I swear ... I *promise* ... simply being yourself is the greatest ...
and the easiest ... freedom that you will ever know.

Over ten years after writing "Starlight", I felt that I had truly come to understand and further comprehend just what I'd been shown in that most mystical dream. I don't want to go into dissecting or further explaining it here.

I don't think it needs that.

It is one of my favorite things that I have ever written and you, dear Reader, can take from it, and "Starlight", anything you wish. It's just that it is one of my more confounding writes and I wanted to share with you why.

I decided to revisit it as another poem. I wanted it to be less imagery (read: cryptic). As you can see, it *started* that way. But for whatever reason, after the first verse, I didn't write it with a rhyme or iambics. It just stopped coming out that way.

When I write, it is "automatic" ... I don't force it out or purposely write it. I just take a concept or idea or influence and "let it rip", as I call it, when it comes to me. I may go back and "sweeten" or rearrange it. I also may add or subtract. But ... 99.5% of what I pen is left exactly as you see it. I just let it out.

I'm not sure why it is this way, it just is.

I can't make myself sit and write something, it has to "come out". I may have an idea or concept and it may be in my head for months or even years and then one day ... boom, there it is. Sometimes I get an idea and I call it "planting a seed". I know I can't write about it at that moment ... but one day ... it will arrive.

This piece has two "firsts" for me ...

One, is that it is the first, and only, time I have ever revisited a previous write and expounded or expressed it more deeply. "Starlight" was written more poetic, more eloquent ... this one, more as an essay or spoken word. I won't call it "free verse" poetry.

As I've mentioned before, I'm a purist, when it comes to that. To me, poetry is poetry. Pure and simple. Yes, the definition does *not* say that it *all* must actually rhyme ... but take that up with Robert Frost.

The second "first", is that it is the first time I ever sat down to write a poem and had it *turn* into an essay. On the first read of it, I shook my head with a grin. It was so odd. But what can ya do? Like I said, I just "Let them rip".

Overall, I guess what I'm trying to say here ... is that "Starlight" was written for me ...

"Celestial" ... is for *you*.

Rise!

Get up!
Get up!
Get on your feet!
Select all your problems and hit delete.
Leap straight up into the sky.
Dream all your dreams and
rise!

Stand up!
Stand up!
Do not stop running!
Right now is the time for courage and cunning.
Nothing is gained unless you try.
Forget all your fears and
rise!

Raise up!
Raise up!
This is your life!
You must remain strong and sharp as a knife.
Keep your hands on the wheel and eyes on the prize.
Rewards are relinquished to those who
rise!

The past is gone.
The future's all that you've got.
Study that timeline and untie the knots.
Opportunity sometimes wears a disguise.
Now go out and find it,
It's time to rise!

Jump up!
Jump up!
Spread your wings!
The more effort you give, the more joy that it brings.
Don't just look around …
Open your eyes!
You only live once!
Now get up and
rise!

I have no idea what made me write this ... or even where it came from. As many do, it just came to me when I was driving a back country road with the radio off. I raced home and, as I say ... "Let it rip".

I love it.

It's a really stirring, empowering and encouraging piece. Maybe I just needed that at that moment. I really don't know. It is kind of structured like a song, but that wasn't intentional.

My mind befuddles me on a constant basis!

I also later remembered that that word had been written in blood on the wall at the Rosemary and Leno LaBianca murder scene by one of Charles Manson's minions ...

Well ... I have stolen it BACK!

Parting Is Such

Sweet Sorrow

Thanks *so* much, dear Reader …
You've no idea what it means to me that you spent this
time here with me … *and* that you took this journey with me.
I hope that I've kept my promise and that
you've found something here.

If so …
Keep it … it's yours.
A gift … from *me* to *you*.

I truly hope it is something that you can treasure or even pass along.

As I told you in the beginning, when we met …
this was a sampler, of sorts.
I have more in the works and I hope beyond hope
that you come back here and our journey can continue!

I *loved* adventuring with you!

And isn't *that* what it's all about?

The adventure to all these amazing destinations?

Iter tutum facete,

~Jeff

Open Credits To Quotes and Lyrics Found Within This Book

The quotes and lyrics used within this book are used under the rules of fair use, I have no claim to any of them, in whole or in part, whatsoever and they are wholly owned by their credited Author(s). They are all presented in Italics, within quotation marks and have their Author's names posted directly beneath them. My own quotes within this book are not Italicized.

Below is a list of them, a source (if possible) and their Author(s), in the order in which they appear in this book. It is my hope that by discovering them here, they will enlighten and educate you, dear Reader, and that you will patronize these amazing writers. They all have much to teach, much to share and much to offer and are some of my favorites.

From the Bob Marley and the Wailers title: "One Love" © Robert Nesta Marley

Quote © Freya Stark – Sourced from the internet

From the Jimmy Buffet title: "A Pirate Looks at Forty" © Jimmy Buffet

From the Bob Seger and the Silver Bullet Band title: "Travelin' Man" © Bob Seger

From the Bob Seger and the Silver Bullet Band title: "Beautiful Loser" © Bob Seger

Quote © Maya Angelou – Sourced from the internet.

From the Ridley Scott feature film: "Blade Runner" - The actual source of these words are uncertain. Online, it is reported that they were rewritten from the original script by Rutger Hauer and not the original from the screenplay writer. So, I am truly unsure. I only know that he says them in a scene in the film. I do know that they do not appear in the original book from where the movie came, entitled "Do Androids Dream of Electric Sheep", by Philip K. Dick.

From the U2 title: "Whose Gonna Ride You Wild Horses?" © Larry Mullin Jr., Bono, The Edge and Adam Clayton

Quote © Neal Donald Walsch – Sourced from the internet.

Quote © Lauryn Hill – Sourced from the internet.

Quote © Fred Rogers – Sourced from the internet.

Quote © Kevin Brockmeie – Sourced from the internet.

From the INXS title: "The Stairs" - © Andrew Farriss and Michael Hutchence

Quote © Trent Shelton – Sourced from the internet.

From the Simon and Garfunkel title: "Bridge over Troubled Water" © Paul Simon

Quote © Amy Marie Walz – Sourced from the internet.

www.ingramcontent.com/pod-product-compliance
Lightning Source LLC
Chambersburg PA
CBHW021219090426
42740CB00006B/280